SPECTRUM®

Math

Grade 7

Spectrum®

An imprint of Carson-Dellosa Publishing LLC
Greensboro, North Carolina

Spectrum®
An imprint of Carson-Dellosa Publishing LLC
P.O. Box 35665
Greensboro, NC 27425 USA

ISBN 978-0-7696-3697-9

11-111147811

Table of Contents Grade 7

Table of Contents, continued

NAME _____

Check What You Know

Whole Numbers

Add, subtract, multiply, or divide.

	a	b	c	d	e
1.	24 68 +53	326 479 +194	7036 1428 + 311	37924 18657 +93214	114738 506247 +382011
2.	74 − 8	325 − 47	8804 −7963	57264 −19896	402685 −237418
3.	17 ×28	473 × 57	3862 × 9	7043 × 6	5877 × 43
4.	43 ×37	648 ×209	829 ×634	2189 × 615	1724 × 568

5. $8\overline{)56}$ $3\overline{)743}$ $5\overline{)3807}$ $66\overline{)794}$ $28\overline{)596}$

6. $71\overline{)934}$ $19\overline{)6118}$ $42\overline{)9527}$ $36\overline{)10379}$ $53\overline{)74891}$

Check What You Know

SHOW YOUR WORK

Whole Numbers

Solve each problem.

7. Manuel read 58 pages on Sunday, 37 pages on Monday, and 43 pages on Tuesday. How many total pages did he read?

Manuel read _____ pages.

8. If a car travels at an average speed of 48 miles per hour, how long will it take to go 1,776 miles?

It will take _____ hours.

9. Kendra earns $63 dollars a week at her part-time job. She plans to work 28 weeks this year. How much money will she earn?

She will earn _____.

10. A factory produced 593,257 calculators. However, 5,728 of them were defective. How many were good?

Of all the calculators, _____ were good.

11. Mr. Fallows bought 3,560 square feet of land. It cost $33 for each square foot. How much did Mr. Fallows spend?

Mr. Fallows spent _____.

12. Mr. Fallows divided his 3,560 square feet of land into 23 equal plots, and he used the rest for a compost pile. How large was each plot? How large was the compost pile?

Each plot was _____ square feet.

The compost pile was _____ square feet.

7.

8.

9.

10.

11.

12.

Lesson 1.1 Adding through 6 Digits

	Add ones.	Add tens.	Add hundreds.
addend	324138	324138	324138
addend	407317	407317	407317
+ addend	+ 62332	+ 62332	+ 62332
sum	7	87	787

	Add thousands.	Add ten thousands.	Add hundred thousands.
	324138	324138	324138
	407317	407317	407317
	+ 62332	+ 62332	+ 62332
	3787	93787	793787

Add.

	a	b	c	d	e
1.	375 + 17	42 +136	526 +417	2248 +13271	642371 +115238
2.	78 +49	341 +406	5583 +2473	78426 + 1381	113471 +207369
3.	53 +928	620 +620	3865 + 927	55371 +40693	849380 + 20618
4.	43 27 +108	126 403 +369	4287 3500 +1124	38257 4126 + 5310	586203 102479 +130592
5.	33 12 60 +14	441 302 124 +113	3121 1407 2242 +1158	13112 20841 33072 +11825	135276 213401 106592 +321145

Lesson 1.2   Subtracting through 6 Digits

	Subtract ones.	Subtract tens.	Subtract hundreds.
minuend	$8\,3\,7\,5\,8\,\overset{7\ 14}{\cancel{8}\cancel{4}}$	$8\,3\,7\,5\,8\,\overset{7\ 14}{\cancel{8}\cancel{4}}$	$8\,3\,7\,\overset{6\ 15\ 7\ 14}{\cancel{5}\cancel{8}\cancel{4}}$
− subtrahend	$-\ 6\,4\,5\,7\,3\,6$	$-\ 6\,4\,5\,7\,3\,6$	$-\ 6\,4\,5\,7\,3\,6$
difference	8	$4\,8$	$8\,4\,8$

	Subtract thousands.	Subtract ten thousands.	Subtract hundred thousands.
	$8\,3\,7\,\overset{6\ 15\ 7\ 14}{\cancel{5}\cancel{8}\cancel{4}}$	$\overset{7\ 13\ 6\ 15\ 7\ 14}{\cancel{8}\,3\,7\,\cancel{5}\cancel{8}\cancel{4}}$	$\overset{7\ 13\ 6\ 15\ 7\ 14}{\cancel{8}\,3\,7\,\cancel{5}\cancel{8}\cancel{4}}$
	$-\ 6\,4\,5\,7\,3\,6$	$-\ 6\,4\,5\,7\,3\,6$	$-\ 6\,4\,5\,7\,3\,6$
	$1\,8\,4\,8$	$9\,1\,8\,4\,8$	$1\,9\,1\,8\,4\,8$

Subtract.

	a	b	c	d	e
1.	38 − 7	629 − 35	4224 − 115	55243 −34127	203798 −121471
2.	44 −28	708 −521	8974 −2187	38719 −16423	932487 −350378
3.	93 − 8	392 − 98	5936 −2852	77259 −39648	832945 − 41858
4.	34 −26	842 −551	7734 −2817	98327 − 9415	438721 −394632
5.	88 −29	487 −338	3381 −2465	64238 − 7156	704632 −464651
6.	62 −39	530 −267	6642 −3951	87403 −29312	384723 − 66905

Lesson 1.3 Problem Solving

SHOW YOUR WORK

Solve each problem.

1. Stu bought a book for $17. He paid with a $20 bill. How much change did he receive?

   Stu received _____ in change.

   1.

2. The populations of Pottsville, Middleton, and Swain are 38,247; 42,635; and 1,324. What is the total population of these cities?

   The total population is _____.

   2.

3. Rosa's car is due for its next service at 150,000 miles. So far she has driven 138,271 miles. How many more miles can she drive until her car needs service?

   She can drive _____ more miles.

   3.

4. A girl's club had a car wash to raise money. The girls made $224 on Friday, $392 on Saturday, and $434 on Sunday. In the three days, how much money did they raise?

   They raised _____.

   4.

5. The stadium has 35,867 seats. Only 26,437 people attended last night's game. How many seats were empty?

   There were _____ empty seats.

   5.

6. In the first four games of the season, the Muskrat basketball team scored 77, 88, 93, and 101 points. How many points did they score in the first 4 games?

   They scored _____ points.

   6.

7. At Gainesville Middle School, there are 327 students in the sixth grade, 463 students in the seventh grade, and 308 students in the eighth grade. How many students are there at Gainesville Middle School?

   There are _____ students at Gainesville Middle School.

   7.

Lesson 1.4 Multiplying through 4 Digits

Multiply 5824 by 7 ones.	Multiply 5824 by 4 tens.	Multiply 5824 by 1 hundred. Then add.
$$\begin{array}{r} {}^{5}{}^{1}{}^{2}\\ 5824 \\ \times\quad 147 \\ \hline 40768 \end{array}$$	$$\begin{array}{r} {}^{3}\;{}^{1}\\ 5824 \\ \times\quad 147 \\ \hline 40768 \\ 232960 \end{array}$$	$$\begin{array}{r} 5824 \\ \times\quad 147 \\ \hline 40768 \\ 232960 \\ +582400 \\ \hline 856128 \end{array}\Big\} \text{Add}$$

Multiply.

	a	b	c	d
1.	$\begin{array}{r} 37 \\ \times\ 4 \\ \hline \end{array}$	$\begin{array}{r} 682 \\ \times\ 7 \\ \hline \end{array}$	$\begin{array}{r} 526 \\ \times\ 3 \\ \hline \end{array}$	$\begin{array}{r} 2173 \\ \times\ 5 \\ \hline \end{array}$
2.	$\begin{array}{r} 46 \\ \times\ 53 \\ \hline \end{array}$	$\begin{array}{r} 376 \\ \times\ 49 \\ \hline \end{array}$	$\begin{array}{r} 423 \\ \times\ 64 \\ \hline \end{array}$	$\begin{array}{r} 5833 \\ \times\ 71 \\ \hline \end{array}$
3.	$\begin{array}{r} 68 \\ \times\ 29 \\ \hline \end{array}$	$\begin{array}{r} 287 \\ \times\ 423 \\ \hline \end{array}$	$\begin{array}{r} 323 \\ \times\ 605 \\ \hline \end{array}$	$\begin{array}{r} 4827 \\ \times\ 356 \\ \hline \end{array}$
4.	$\begin{array}{r} 37 \\ \times\ 468 \\ \hline \end{array}$	$\begin{array}{r} 732 \\ \times\ 268 \\ \hline \end{array}$	$\begin{array}{r} 3371 \\ \times\ 340 \\ \hline \end{array}$	$\begin{array}{r} 2479 \\ \times\ 236 \\ \hline \end{array}$

Lesson 1.5   Dividing by 1 Digit

Divide 275 by 8.

$$
\begin{array}{r}
3 \\
8\overline{)275} \\
-240 \\
\hline
35
\end{array}
$$

$30 \times 8 = 240$

subtract.

Divide 35 by 8.

$$
\begin{array}{r}
34\,r3 \\
8\overline{)275} \\
-240 \\
\hline
35 \\
-32 \\
\hline
3
\end{array}
$$

$4 \times 8 = 32$

subtract.

$3 < 8$, so it is a remainder.

Divide.

	a	b	c	d	e
1.	$7\overline{)43}$	$3\overline{)87}$	$4\overline{)215}$	$6\overline{)408}$	$3\overline{)2334}$
2.	$9\overline{)83}$	$2\overline{)75}$	$5\overline{)427}$	$7\overline{)3804}$	$6\overline{)1037}$
3.	$4\overline{)56}$	$7\overline{)123}$	$3\overline{)526}$	$2\overline{)4129}$	$4\overline{)7723}$

Lesson 1.6 Dividing by 2 Digits

Divide 39 by 17.

$$\begin{array}{r} 2 \\ 17\overline{)392} \\ -340 \\ \hline 52 \end{array}$$ 20 × 17 = 340
        subtract.

Divide 52 by 17.

$$\begin{array}{r} 23\,r\,1 \\ 17\overline{)392} \\ -340 \\ \hline 52 \\ -51 \\ \hline 1 \end{array}$$ 3 × 17 = 51
        subtract.

1 < 17, so it is a remainder.

Divide.

	a	b	c	d	e
1.	12$\overline{)409}$	26$\overline{)722}$	43$\overline{)159}$	72$\overline{)518}$	63$\overline{)741}$
2.	37$\overline{)984}$	51$\overline{)348}$	16$\overline{)614}$	83$\overline{)265}$	98$\overline{)686}$
3.	44$\overline{)820}$	14$\overline{)322}$	54$\overline{)329}$	28$\overline{)937}$	31$\overline{)835}$

Lesson 1.6 Dividing by 2 Digits

Divide 78 by 23.

$$23\overline{)78443}$$
$$\quad\ \ 3$$
$$\ -69 \qquad 3 \times 23 = 69$$
$$\ \ \overline{9443}\ \text{ subtract.}$$

Divide 94 by 23.

$$23\overline{)78443}$$
$$\quad\ \ 34$$
$$\ -69$$
$$\ \ \overline{9443}$$
$$\ -92 \qquad 4 \times 23 = 92$$
$$\ \ \overline{243}\ \text{ subtract.}$$

Divide 24 by 23.

$$23\overline{)78443}$$
$$\quad\ \ 3410\ r13$$
$$\ -69$$
$$\ \ \overline{9443}$$
$$\ -92$$
$$\ \ \overline{243}$$
$$\ -23 \qquad 1 \times 23 = 23$$
$$\ \ \overline{13}\ \text{ subtract.}$$

13 < 23, so the ones digit is 0 and 13 is a remainder.

Divide.

	a	b	c	d	e
1.	$14\overline{)3827}$	$72\overline{)6839}$	$35\overline{)21210}$	$49\overline{)61738}$	$62\overline{)39426}$
2.	$25\overline{)4417}$	$41\overline{)9717}$	$53\overline{)11208}$	$26\overline{)59324}$	$12\overline{)77139}$
3.	$38\overline{)9462}$	$54\overline{)5831}$	$81\overline{)30498}$	$97\overline{)98417}$	$73\overline{)32631}$

Lesson 1.7 Problem Solving

Solve each problem.

1. Jackie expects 327 people at her banquet. She noticed that there are 48 napkins in a package. How many full packages of napkins will she need? How many napkins will be left?

   Jackie will need _____ full packages and _____ napkins will be left.

2. The auditorium has 175 rows of seats. Each row has 54 seats. How many seats are there in the auditorium?

   There are _____ seats in the auditorium.

3. The school collected 48,251 box tops. If each student brought in exactly 113 box tops, how many students are in the school?

   There are _____ students in the school.

4. An average of 326 cars drive over the Rollins Bridge every day. How many cars drive over the bridge each year (365 days)?

   Each year, _____ cars drive over the bridge.

5. Luisa's car goes 24 miles on a gallon of gas. How many gallons of gas will she need to drive 1,128 miles?

   Luisa will need _____ gallons of gas.

6. There are 5,280 feet in a mile. If it is 127 miles from Danville to Center City, how many feet apart are the two cities?

   The two cities are _____ feet apart.

7. Marcus needs 448 bricks for a construction project. He can buy bricks in cases of 72. How many cases does he need to buy? How many extra bricks will he have?

   He needs to buy _____ cases, and he will have _____ extra bricks.

1.

2.

3.

4.

5.

6.

7.

Check What You Learned

Whole Numbers

Add, subtract, multiply, or divide.

	a	b	c	d	e
1.	39 46 +88	527 650 +396	6824 5173 +2051	33623 97046 +81997	732448 196823 +243599
2.	91 − 7	539 − 96	3510 −1906	74237 −58246	656043 −278126
3.	44 ×68	731 × 96	1328 × 6	5744 × 3	2108 × 18
4.	83 ×91	632 ×570	812 ×348	2436 × 291	1509 × 854

5. $6\overline{)73}$ $\quad$ $4\overline{)891}$ $\quad$ $3\overline{)5752}$ $\quad$ $23\overline{)560}$ $\quad$ $49\overline{)642}$

6. $63\overline{)5927}$ $\quad$ $26\overline{)7244}$ $\quad$ $37\overline{)4128}$ $\quad$ $94\overline{)38249}$ $\quad$ $78\overline{)27378}$

Check What You Learned

SHOW YOUR WORK

Whole Numbers

Solve each problem.

7. There were 343 men, 427 women, and 856 children at the carnival. What was the total attendance?

There were _____ people in attendance.

7.

8. Olivia and Steve baked 22 batches of cookies for the bake sale. Each batch had 36 cookies. How many cookies did they bake?

They baked _____ cookies.

8.

9. Maria needed to send out 237 invitations. She bought stamps in books of 20 and then bought extra stamps individually. How many books of stamps did she buy? How many extra stamps did she have to buy?

She had to buy _____ books and _____ extra stamps.

9.

10. It is 4,382 feet around the lower walking track at the park. It is 2,747 feet around the upper track. How much longer is the lower track than the upper track?

The lower track is _____ feet longer.

10.

11. A team of 5 runners competed in a relay race. Each runner had to run 730 yards. How long was the race?

The race was _____ yards long.

11.

12. A factory manufactures 68,424 parts a day. The factory operates 24 hours a day and makes the same number of parts each hour. How many parts does it make in an hour?

It makes _____ parts in an hour.

12.

NAME _____

Check What You Know

Fractions

Add, subtract, multiply, or divide. Write each answer in simplest form.

	a	**b**	**c**	**d**
1.	$2\frac{1}{4}$ $+2\frac{2}{3}$	$3\frac{1}{2}$ $+2\frac{1}{7}$	$2\frac{1}{8}$ $+4\frac{2}{3}$	$1\frac{5}{7}$ $+2\frac{4}{5}$
2.	$6\frac{1}{3}$ $-2\frac{1}{4}$	$\frac{3}{8}$ $-\frac{1}{4}$	$5\frac{3}{10}$ $-2\frac{4}{5}$	$3\frac{4}{7}$ $-1\frac{1}{2}$
3.	$\frac{3}{4} \times \frac{1}{6}$	$\frac{5}{7} \times \frac{2}{3}$	$\frac{1}{2} \times \frac{4}{9}$	$\frac{7}{10} \times \frac{3}{8} \times \frac{1}{4}$
4.	$2\frac{1}{3} \times 1\frac{3}{8}$	$5\frac{1}{2} \times 1\frac{1}{4}$	$3\frac{3}{7} \times 1\frac{5}{6}$	$3\frac{1}{4} \times 1\frac{1}{3} \times \frac{1}{2}$
5.	$5\frac{1}{4} \div 1\frac{3}{8}$	$6\frac{4}{7} \div 12$	$1\frac{1}{2} \div \frac{3}{5}$	$2\frac{2}{3} \div 3\frac{1}{6}$

NAME _____

Check What You Know

Fractions

Solve each problem.

6. One box of clips weighs $4\frac{2}{3}$ ounces. Another box weighs $5\frac{3}{8}$ ounces. What is the total weight of the two boxes?

The total weight is _____ ounces.

6.

7. Luggage on a certain airline is limited to 2 pieces per person. Together the 2 pieces can weigh no more than $58\frac{1}{2}$ pounds. If a passenger has one piece of luggage that weighs $32\frac{1}{3}$ pounds, what is the most the second piece can weigh?

The second piece can weigh _____ pounds.

7.

8. Mavis spends $1\frac{1}{4}$ hours on the bus every weekday (Monday through Friday). How many hours is she on the bus each week?

She is on the bus _____ hours each week.

8.

9. A bucket that holds $5\frac{1}{4}$ gallons of water is being used to fill a tub that can hold $34\frac{1}{8}$ gallons. How many buckets will be needed to fill the tub?

_____ buckets are needed to fill the tub.

9.

10. A black piece of pipe is $8\frac{1}{3}$ centimeters long. A silver piece of pipe is $2\frac{3}{5}$ times longer. How long is the silver piece of pipe?

The silver piece is _____ centimeters long.

10.

11. One section of wood is $3\frac{5}{8}$ meters long. Another section is $5\frac{2}{3}$ meters. When the two pieces are put together to make a single piece, how long is the piece of wood?

The piece of wood is _____ meters long.

11.

Lesson 2.1   Finding the Greatest Common Factor

$16 = 1 \times 16, \ 2 \times 8, \ 4 \times 4$ ①, ②, ④, ⑧, and 16 are factors.

$24 = 1 \times 24, \ 2 \times 12, \ 3 \times 8, \ 4 \times 6$ ①, ②, 3, ④, 6, ⑧, 12, 24 are factors.

The common factors of **16** and **24** are circled.

The greatest common factor is **8**.

List the factors of each number shown below.
Then, list the common factors and greatest common factor.

		Factors	**Common Factor(s)**	**Greatest Common Factor**
1.	14	1, 2, 7, 14		
	21	1, 3, 7, 21	1, 7	7
2.	12			
	20			
3.	10			
	12			
4.	24			
	36			
5.	9			
	15			
6.	6			
	8			
7.	18			
	20			

Lesson 2.2   Reducing to Simplest Form

A fraction is in simplest form when the greatest common factor of the numerator and denominator is 1. A mixed numeral is in simplest form when its fraction is in simplest form and has a value between 0 and 1. Divide the numerator and denominator by their greatest common factor.

$$\frac{6}{12} = \frac{6 \div 6}{12 \div 6} = \frac{1}{2} \qquad\qquad 7\frac{14}{21} = \frac{14 \div 7}{21 \div 7} = 7\frac{2}{3}$$

Write each of the following in simplest form.

	a	b	c
1.	$\frac{18}{20}$	$3\frac{18}{24}$	$\frac{25}{95}$
2.	$\frac{14}{28}$	$\frac{36}{40}$	$9\frac{8}{12}$
3.	$\frac{36}{48}$	$7\frac{4}{12}$	$\frac{27}{36}$
4.	$8\frac{9}{12}$	$6\frac{5}{20}$	$4\frac{50}{70}$
5.	$4\frac{3}{15}$	$\frac{16}{32}$	$2\frac{12}{52}$

Lesson 2.3   Finding Common Denominators

The **least common multiple (LCM)** is the smallest multiple that is shared by two numbers. Rename fractions so they have common denominators by finding the LCM of the denominators.

$\frac{1}{2}$ and $\frac{2}{3}$ do not have common denominators. The LCM of 2 and 3 is 6.

$$\frac{1}{2} \times \frac{3}{3} = \frac{3}{6} \qquad\qquad \frac{2}{3} \times \frac{2}{2} = \frac{4}{6}$$

$\frac{3}{6}$ and $\frac{4}{6}$ do have common denominators.

Find the LCM and rename each pair of fractions with common denominators.

	a	**b**
1.	$\frac{1}{6}$ and $\frac{2}{5}$ _____	$\frac{3}{8}$ and $\frac{1}{3}$ _____
2.	$\frac{3}{4}$ and $\frac{1}{7}$ _____	$\frac{1}{6}$ and $\frac{3}{4}$ _____
3.	$\frac{1}{2}$ and $\frac{5}{8}$ _____	$\frac{1}{4}$ and $\frac{3}{10}$ _____
4.	$\frac{1}{5}$ and $\frac{4}{9}$ _____	$\frac{2}{5}$ and $\frac{1}{4}$ _____
5.	$\frac{1}{3}$ and $\frac{3}{5}$ _____	$\frac{1}{6}$ and $\frac{2}{9}$ _____

Lesson 2.4 Renaming Fractions and Mixed Numerals

Every whole number can be written as a fraction with a denominator of 1.

$$3 = \frac{3}{1} \qquad 10 = \frac{10}{1} \qquad 25 = \frac{25}{1}$$

Change $2\frac{3}{4}$ to a fraction.

$$2\frac{3}{4} = \frac{2}{1} + \frac{3}{4} = \frac{2 \times 4}{4} + \frac{3}{4}$$
$$= \frac{8 + 3}{4} = \frac{11}{4}$$

Change $\frac{15}{6}$ to a mixed numeral.

$$\frac{15}{6} = 6\overline{)15} = 2\frac{3}{6} = 2\frac{1}{2}$$
$$\frac{-12}{3}$$

Change each of the following to a fraction. Reduce to simplest form.

	a	b	c	d
1.	$3\frac{5}{8}$	9	$2\frac{3}{7}$	$5\frac{1}{2}$
2.	$1\frac{2}{16}$	$8\frac{3}{12}$	14	$3\frac{5}{6}$
3.	$4\frac{1}{3}$	$4\frac{7}{9}$	$1\frac{2}{5}$	47

Change each of the following to a mixed numeral in simplest form.

	a	b	c	d
4.	$\frac{10}{3}$	$\frac{23}{8}$	$\frac{9}{6}$	$\frac{39}{7}$
5.	$\frac{15}{4}$	$3\frac{8}{3}$	$\frac{18}{12}$	$5\frac{5}{3}$
6.	$\frac{19}{11}$	$\frac{42}{10}$	$7\frac{12}{5}$	$\frac{52}{11}$

Lesson 2.5 Adding and Subtracting Fractions

To add or subtract when the denominators are different, rename the fractions so the denominators are the same.

$$\begin{array}{r}\frac{2}{3}\\+\ \frac{3}{7}\\\hline\end{array} = \begin{array}{r}\frac{2}{3}\times\frac{7}{7}\\+\ \frac{3}{7}\times\frac{3}{3}\\\hline\end{array} = \begin{array}{r}\frac{14}{21}\\+\ \frac{9}{21}\\\hline\frac{23}{21} = 1\frac{2}{21}\end{array}$$

$$\begin{array}{r}\frac{4}{5}\\-\ \frac{1}{10}\\\hline\end{array} = \begin{array}{r}\frac{4}{5}\times\frac{2}{2}\\-\ \frac{1}{10}\\\hline\end{array} = \begin{array}{r}\frac{8}{10}\\-\ \frac{1}{10}\\\hline\frac{7}{10}\end{array}$$

Write each answer in simplest form.

	a	b	c	d
1.	$\begin{array}{r}\frac{3}{4}\\+\ \frac{5}{8}\\\hline\end{array}$	$\begin{array}{r}\frac{1}{2}\\+\ \frac{1}{3}\\\hline\end{array}$	$\begin{array}{r}\frac{3}{4}\\+\ \frac{2}{5}\\\hline\end{array}$	$\begin{array}{r}\frac{1}{6}\\+\ \frac{1}{3}\\\hline\end{array}$
2.	$\begin{array}{r}\frac{3}{8}\\+\ \frac{4}{5}\\\hline\end{array}$	$\begin{array}{r}\frac{1}{2}\\+\ \frac{3}{10}\\\hline\end{array}$	$\begin{array}{r}\frac{2}{3}\\+\ \frac{3}{12}\\\hline\end{array}$	$\begin{array}{r}\frac{3}{4}\\+\ \frac{7}{10}\\\hline\end{array}$
3.	$\begin{array}{r}\frac{1}{4}\\+\ \frac{3}{8}\\\hline\end{array}$	$\begin{array}{r}\frac{2}{5}\\+\ \frac{3}{7}\\\hline\end{array}$	$\begin{array}{r}\frac{1}{7}\\+\ \frac{7}{8}\\\hline\end{array}$	$\begin{array}{r}\frac{2}{3}\\+\ \frac{1}{5}\\\hline\end{array}$
4.	$\begin{array}{r}\frac{3}{5}\\-\ \frac{1}{4}\\\hline\end{array}$	$\begin{array}{r}\frac{1}{2}\\-\ \frac{3}{10}\\\hline\end{array}$	$\begin{array}{r}\frac{7}{8}\\-\ \frac{1}{2}\\\hline\end{array}$	$\begin{array}{r}\frac{4}{5}\\-\ \frac{1}{3}\\\hline\end{array}$
5.	$\begin{array}{r}\frac{5}{6}\\-\ \frac{1}{3}\\\hline\end{array}$	$\begin{array}{r}\frac{2}{3}\\-\ \frac{1}{5}\\\hline\end{array}$	$\begin{array}{r}\frac{5}{8}\\-\ \frac{1}{6}\\\hline\end{array}$	$\begin{array}{r}\frac{7}{10}\\-\ \frac{1}{2}\\\hline\end{array}$
6.	$\begin{array}{r}\frac{3}{4}\\-\ \frac{2}{3}\\\hline\end{array}$	$\begin{array}{r}\frac{5}{9}\\-\ \frac{1}{2}\\\hline\end{array}$	$\begin{array}{r}\frac{1}{2}\\-\ \frac{1}{3}\\\hline\end{array}$	$\begin{array}{r}\frac{7}{11}\\-\ \frac{2}{9}\\\hline\end{array}$

Lesson 2.6   Adding and Subtracting Mixed Numerals

To add or subtract mixed numerals when the denominators of the fractions are different, find a common denominator and rename the fractions.

$$3\tfrac{1}{2} = 3\tfrac{3}{6}$$
$$+2\tfrac{2}{3} = +2\tfrac{4}{6}$$
$$5\tfrac{7}{6} = 6\tfrac{1}{6}$$

$$4\tfrac{1}{4} = 4\tfrac{1}{4} = 3\tfrac{5}{4}$$
$$-2\tfrac{1}{2} = -2\tfrac{2}{4} = -2\tfrac{2}{4}$$
$$1\tfrac{3}{4}$$

Write each answer in simplest form.

	a	b	c	d
1.	$1\tfrac{1}{3}$ $+2\tfrac{1}{4}$	$3\tfrac{3}{8}$ $+7\tfrac{1}{2}$	$4\tfrac{2}{7}$ $+2\tfrac{1}{3}$	$1\tfrac{2}{5}$ $+3\tfrac{3}{10}$
2.	$4\tfrac{4}{9}$ $+3\tfrac{1}{3}$	$1\tfrac{1}{8}$ $+1\tfrac{7}{10}$	$2\tfrac{1}{6}$ $+3\tfrac{5}{8}$	$1\tfrac{3}{7}$ $+2\tfrac{1}{5}$
3.	$3\tfrac{1}{2}$ $+2\tfrac{1}{4}$	$2\tfrac{5}{6}$ $+1\tfrac{5}{9}$	$3\tfrac{4}{7}$ $+1\tfrac{1}{10}$	$4\tfrac{1}{3}$ $+2\tfrac{1}{2}$
4.	$2\tfrac{3}{8}$ $-1\tfrac{2}{9}$	$3\tfrac{1}{4}$ $-1\tfrac{1}{3}$	$4\tfrac{1}{2}$ $-3\tfrac{3}{4}$	$6\tfrac{5}{8}$ $-4\tfrac{6}{7}$
5.	$3\tfrac{2}{11}$ $-1\tfrac{5}{8}$	$7\tfrac{2}{3}$ $-3\tfrac{2}{5}$	$5\tfrac{1}{3}$ $-2\tfrac{1}{2}$	$2\tfrac{5}{6}$ $-1\tfrac{2}{7}$
6.	$4\tfrac{7}{9}$ $-2\tfrac{2}{3}$	$3\tfrac{1}{5}$ $-1\tfrac{3}{4}$	$4\tfrac{5}{6}$ $-2\tfrac{1}{8}$	$3\tfrac{1}{8}$ $-1\tfrac{3}{4}$

Lesson 2.7   Problem Solving

Solve each problem.

1. At closing time, the bakery had $2\frac{1}{4}$ apple pies and $1\frac{1}{2}$ cherry pies left. How much more apple pie than cherry pie was left?

   There was _____ more of an apple pie than cherry.

   1.

2. The hardware store sold $6\frac{3}{8}$ boxes of large nails and $7\frac{2}{5}$ boxes of small nails. In total, how many boxes of nails did the store sell?

   The store sold _____ boxes of nails.

   2.

3. Nita studied $4\frac{1}{3}$ hours on Saturday and $5\frac{1}{4}$ hours on Sunday. How many hours did she spend studying?

   She spent _____ hours studying.

   3.

4. Kwan is $5\frac{2}{3}$ feet tall. Mary is $4\frac{11}{12}$ feet tall. How much taller is Kwan?

   Kwan is _____ foot taller.

   4.

5. This week, Jim practiced the piano $1\frac{1}{8}$ hours on Monday and $2\frac{3}{7}$ hours on Tuesday. How many hours did he practice this week? How much longer did Jim practice on Tuesday than on Monday?

   Jim practiced _____ hours this week.

   Jim practiced _____ hours longer on Tuesday.

   5.

6. Oscar caught a fish that weighed $4\frac{1}{6}$ pounds and then caught another that weighed $6\frac{5}{8}$ pounds. How much more did the second fish weigh?

   The second fish weighed _____ pounds more.

   6.

NAME _____

Lesson 2.8   Multiplying Fractions

Reduce to simplest form if possible. Then, multiply the numerators and multiply the denominators.

$$\frac{3}{8} \times \frac{5}{6} \times \frac{1}{7} = \frac{\overset{1}{\cancel{3}} \times 5 \times 1}{8 \times \underset{2}{\cancel{6}} \times 7} = \frac{1 \times 5 \times 1}{8 \times 2 \times 7} = \frac{5}{112}$$

Write each answer in simplest form.

	a	b	c	d
1.	$\frac{1}{2} \times \frac{3}{4}$	$\frac{2}{3} \times \frac{4}{5}$	$\frac{3}{4} \times \frac{3}{4}$	$\frac{4}{5} \times \frac{1}{8}$
2.	$\frac{3}{5} \times \frac{7}{8}$	$\frac{1}{3} \times \frac{3}{5}$	$\frac{3}{7} \times \frac{1}{5}$	$\frac{3}{10} \times \frac{4}{5}$
3.	$\frac{5}{8} \times \frac{3}{8}$	$\frac{2}{3} \times \frac{1}{2}$	$\frac{5}{6} \times \frac{2}{3}$	$\frac{4}{7} \times \frac{1}{3}$
4.	$\frac{1}{2} \times \frac{1}{3} \times \frac{2}{3}$	$\frac{2}{3} \times \frac{3}{5} \times \frac{1}{2}$	$\frac{2}{3} \times \frac{4}{5} \times \frac{2}{7}$	$\frac{1}{3} \times \frac{5}{8} \times \frac{1}{2}$
5.	$\frac{1}{4} \times \frac{3}{4} \times \frac{1}{2}$	$\frac{1}{3} \times \frac{3}{4} \times \frac{1}{2}$	$\frac{3}{7} \times \frac{2}{3} \times \frac{3}{4}$	$\frac{5}{8} \times \frac{2}{3} \times \frac{1}{5}$
6.	$\frac{3}{7} \times \frac{1}{2} \times \frac{2}{5}$	$\frac{4}{9} \times \frac{3}{5} \times \frac{1}{8}$	$\frac{7}{8} \times \frac{2}{5} \times \frac{1}{3}$	$\frac{4}{5} \times \frac{3}{4} \times \frac{5}{8}$

Lesson 2.9 Multiplying Mixed Numerals

Rename the numbers as fractions. Reduce to simplest form. Multiply the numerators and denominators. Simplify.

$$3\frac{1}{5} \times 2\frac{2}{3} \times 1\frac{1}{8} = \frac{16 \times \overset{1}{\cancel{8}} \times \overset{3}{\cancel{9}}}{5 \times \underset{1}{\cancel{3}} \times \underset{1}{\cancel{8}}} = \frac{16 \times 1 \times 3}{5 \times 1 \times 1} = \frac{48}{5} = 9\frac{3}{5}$$

Write each answer in simplest form.

	a	**b**	**c**
1.	$3 \times 1\frac{2}{7}$	$2\frac{1}{4} \times 3\frac{1}{3}$	$1\frac{1}{9} \times 3\frac{1}{4}$
2.	$2\frac{1}{4} \times 6$	$1\frac{2}{3} \times 3\frac{7}{8}$	$2\frac{1}{7} \times 1\frac{1}{3}$
3.	$4\frac{1}{2} \times 2\frac{1}{3} \times 3$	$5\frac{1}{4} \times 2\frac{1}{2} \times 1\frac{1}{3}$	$4\frac{1}{8} \times 3\frac{2}{7} \times 7$
4.	$\frac{5}{6} \times 1\frac{1}{3} \times 2$	$\frac{2}{3} \times 1\frac{5}{8} \times 3\frac{1}{4}$	$1\frac{1}{2} \times 2\frac{2}{3} \times 1\frac{1}{8}$
5.	$2\frac{1}{4} \times 1\frac{1}{8} \times \frac{2}{3}$	$\frac{5}{6} \times 1\frac{3}{8} \times 2\frac{2}{3}$	$2\frac{1}{4} \times 1\frac{1}{3} \times 1\frac{2}{9}$
6.	$5 \times 1\frac{1}{7} \times 2\frac{1}{5}$	$1\frac{1}{7} \times \frac{5}{8} \times 2\frac{1}{3}$	$1\frac{1}{9} \times \frac{3}{8} \times 2\frac{1}{3}$

Lesson 2.10   Reciprocals

Any two numbers with a product of 1 are reciprocals.

$\frac{3}{4} \times \frac{4}{3} = \frac{12}{12} = 1$

$\frac{3}{4}$ and $\frac{4}{3}$ are reciprocals.

$1\frac{3}{4} \times \frac{4}{7} = \frac{7}{4} \times \frac{4}{7} = \frac{28}{28} = 1$

$1\frac{3}{4}$ (or $\frac{7}{4}$) and $\frac{4}{7}$ are reciprocals.

Write the reciprocal.

	a	b	c	d	e	f
1.	$\frac{2}{3}$ _____	$1\frac{1}{8}$ _____	$\frac{7}{2}$ _____	$3\frac{1}{4}$ _____	$\frac{9}{12}$ _____	$\frac{2}{5}$ _____
2.	$\frac{7}{8}$ _____	$3\frac{1}{3}$ _____	$1\frac{3}{5}$ _____	12 _____	$\frac{3}{7}$ _____	$\frac{1}{2}$ _____
3.	$\frac{1}{10}$ _____	$\frac{3}{5}$ _____	$2\frac{1}{7}$ _____	$\frac{3}{11}$ _____	$2\frac{3}{8}$ _____	4 _____
4.	$\frac{3}{8}$ _____	$\frac{2}{7}$ _____	$\frac{4}{9}$ _____	$1\frac{3}{4}$ _____	$\frac{7}{12}$ _____	$\frac{3}{14}$ _____
5.	$\frac{2}{17}$ _____	$\frac{1}{15}$ _____	$\frac{13}{20}$ _____	$2\frac{2}{9}$ _____	3 _____	$3\frac{4}{7}$ _____
6.	5 _____	$2\frac{1}{2}$ _____	$\frac{3}{5}$ _____	$1\frac{1}{12}$ _____	$1\frac{3}{11}$ _____	$\frac{3}{16}$ _____
7.	$2\frac{3}{7}$ _____	20 _____	$\frac{8}{9}$ _____	$3\frac{5}{16}$ _____	$2\frac{1}{8}$ _____	$\frac{1}{16}$ _____

Lesson 2.11 Dividing Fractions and Mixed Numerals

To divide by a fraction, multiply by its reciprocal.

$$\frac{2}{3} \div \frac{5}{8} = \frac{2}{3} \times \frac{8}{5} = \frac{16}{15} = 1\frac{1}{15} \qquad\qquad 1\frac{2}{3} \div 2\frac{5}{9} = \frac{5}{3} \times \frac{\overset{3}{\cancel{9}}}{23} = \frac{15}{23}$$

Write each answer in simplest form.

	a	b	c	d
1.	$3\frac{1}{2} \div \frac{2}{3}$	$4\frac{3}{4} \div 1\frac{7}{8}$	$\frac{3}{4} \div \frac{1}{2}$	$2\frac{2}{3} \div \frac{1}{8}$
2.	$7 \div \frac{3}{5}$	$2\frac{1}{12} \div 1\frac{1}{3}$	$2\frac{1}{7} \div \frac{3}{4}$	$3 \div 5$
3.	$1\frac{1}{8} \div \frac{1}{10}$	$1\frac{2}{5} \div 2\frac{1}{3}$	$5 \div 1\frac{1}{2}$	$3\frac{1}{4} \div 1\frac{1}{2}$
4.	$6\frac{2}{3} \div \frac{2}{3}$	$3\frac{1}{8} \div \frac{2}{7}$	$4\frac{1}{4} \div \frac{1}{12}$	$14 \div \frac{1}{7}$
5.	$2\frac{3}{5} \div 1\frac{2}{7}$	$1\frac{1}{9} \div \frac{7}{11}$	$12 \div 15$	$2\frac{4}{5} \div 3$

Lesson 2.11 Dividing Fractions and Mixed Numerals

Write each answer in simplest form.

	a	b	c	d
1.	$5\frac{5}{8} \div 2\frac{1}{4}$	$3\frac{4}{7} \div 2\frac{1}{8}$	$3\frac{5}{12} \div 2\frac{1}{6}$	$5\frac{1}{4} \div 3$
2.	$8 \div 17$	$3\frac{9}{10} \div \frac{6}{15}$	$2\frac{1}{4} \div \frac{3}{8}$	$\frac{2}{3} \div \frac{5}{7}$
3.	$\frac{9}{11} \div \frac{3}{8}$	$2\frac{5}{9} \div 1\frac{1}{3}$	$3\frac{5}{12} \div 1\frac{5}{6}$	$1\frac{7}{8} \div \frac{1}{16}$
4.	$4\frac{5}{12} \div 2\frac{3}{4}$	$8 \div \frac{2}{7}$	$4\frac{1}{2} \div 5$	$3\frac{4}{7} \div \frac{5}{8}$
5.	$4\frac{1}{4} \div \frac{7}{10}$	$\frac{2}{11} \div \frac{4}{17}$	$3\frac{3}{8} \div 2$	$5\frac{1}{2} \div 2\frac{1}{3}$
6.	$\frac{7}{8} \div 3$	$6 \div \frac{1}{5}$	$2\frac{4}{9} \div \frac{5}{6}$	$7\frac{1}{4} \div 1\frac{7}{8}$

Lesson 2.12 Multiplication and Division Practice

Write each answer in simplest form.

	a	b	c	d
1.	$\frac{1}{3} \times \frac{3}{8}$	$\frac{7}{6} \times \frac{4}{13}$	$\frac{3}{7} \times \frac{4}{5}$	$\frac{2}{3} \times \frac{1}{2} \times \frac{3}{8}$
2.	$\frac{1}{2} \times \frac{5}{12}$	$\frac{2}{3} \times \frac{5}{9}$	$\frac{1}{8} \times \frac{2}{7} \times \frac{5}{6}$	$\frac{3}{5} \times \frac{2}{3} \times \frac{1}{2}$
3.	$\frac{1}{2} \times 1\frac{2}{5}$	$\frac{5}{7} \times 2\frac{1}{8}$	$1\frac{1}{2} \times 2\frac{1}{4} \times \frac{1}{3}$	$3\frac{1}{8} \times 4\frac{1}{4} \times \frac{1}{3}$
4.	$3\frac{1}{3} \times \frac{1}{4}$	$1\frac{5}{8} \times 2\frac{1}{3}$	$3\frac{4}{7} \times 1\frac{4}{5} \times 2$	$3\frac{1}{4} \times 2\frac{1}{8} \times 1\frac{5}{7}$
5.	$\frac{3}{5} \div \frac{2}{7}$	$\frac{3}{4} \div \frac{1}{2}$	$\frac{5}{8} \div \frac{3}{5}$	$\frac{5}{6} \div \frac{1}{10}$
6.	$5 \div 1\frac{1}{4}$	$3\frac{1}{2} \div \frac{2}{3}$	$1\frac{6}{7} \div 2\frac{1}{8}$	$3\frac{1}{4} \div 2$
7.	$3\frac{7}{10} \div 2\frac{1}{4}$	$5\frac{1}{2} \div 3\frac{6}{11}$	$2\frac{3}{5} \div 13$	$7\frac{1}{4} \div 3\frac{3}{8}$

Lesson 2.13　Problem Solving

Solve each problem. Write each answer in simplest form.

1. David worked $7\frac{1}{3}$ hours today and planted 11 trees. It takes him about the same amount of time to plant each tree. How long did it take him to plant each tree?

   It took him _____ hour to plant each tree.

2. A car uses $3\frac{1}{8}$ gallons of gasoline per hour when driving on the highway. How many gallons will it use after $4\frac{2}{3}$ hours?

   It will use _____ gallons.

3. A board was $24\frac{3}{8}$ inches long. A worker cut it into pieces that were $4\frac{7}{8}$ inches long. The worker cut the board into how many pieces?

   The worker cut the board into _____ pieces.

4. Susan must pour $6\frac{1}{2}$ bottles of juice into 26 drink glasses for her party. If each glass gets the same amount of juice, what fraction of a bottle will each glass hold?

   Each glass will hold _____ bottle.

5. The standard size of a certain bin holds $2\frac{2}{3}$ gallons. The large size of that bin is $1\frac{1}{4}$ times larger. How many gallons does the large bin hold?

   The large bin holds _____ gallons.

6. Diana has $3\frac{1}{4}$ bags of nuts. Each bag holds $4\frac{1}{2}$ pounds. How many pounds of nuts does Diana have?

   Diana has _____ pounds of nuts.

7. There is a stack of 7 crates. Each crate is $10\frac{2}{3}$ inches high. How many inches high is the stack of crates?

   The stack of crates is _____ inches high.

1.

2.

3.

4.

5.

6.

7.

Check What You Learned

Fractions

Add, subtract, multiply, or divide. Write each answer in simplest form.

	a	**b**	**c**	**d**
1.	$\frac{3}{8}$ $+1\frac{5}{7}$	$2\frac{1}{4}$ $+3\frac{1}{3}$	$1\frac{5}{6}$ $+2\frac{7}{8}$	$4\frac{3}{4}$ $+2\frac{3}{8}$
2.	$4\frac{2}{3}$ $-1\frac{1}{4}$	$\frac{7}{8}$ $-\frac{1}{2}$	$4\frac{3}{10}$ $-1\frac{6}{7}$	$5\frac{1}{4}$ $-2\frac{5}{6}$
3.	$\frac{3}{8} \times \frac{4}{5}$	$\frac{1}{2} \times \frac{3}{7}$	$\frac{5}{9} \times \frac{1}{3}$	$\frac{2}{3} \times \frac{1}{4} \times \frac{1}{8}$
4.	$3\frac{2}{7} \times \frac{5}{8}$	$2\frac{3}{4} \times 1\frac{2}{7}$	$3\frac{2}{3} \times 1\frac{5}{6}$	$2\frac{1}{3} \times 1\frac{1}{2} \times 3$
5.	$6\frac{1}{8} \div 2\frac{4}{7}$	$3\frac{2}{3} \div 8$	$5\frac{1}{2} \div 1\frac{2}{5}$	$\frac{3}{4} \div \frac{1}{8}$

Check What You Learned

Fractions

Solve each problem. Write each answer in simplest form.

6. A large patio brick weighs $4\frac{3}{8}$ pounds. A small patio brick weighs $2\frac{1}{3}$ pounds. How much more does the large brick weigh?

The large brick weighs _____ pounds more.

6.

7. A ribbon that is $22\frac{3}{4}$ inches long must be cut into 7 equal pieces. How long will each piece be?

Each piece will be _____ inches long.

7.

8. Fifteen cups of flour are to be stored in containers. Each container holds $2\frac{1}{3}$ cups. How many containers will the flour fill? What fraction of another container will it fill?

The flour will fill _____ full containers and

_____ of another container.

8.

9. A small bottle holds $\frac{1}{3}$ of a liter. A large bottle holds $4\frac{1}{2}$ times as much. How many liters does the large bottle hold?

The large bottle holds _____ liters.

9.

10. The basketball team practiced $3\frac{1}{4}$ hours on Monday and $2\frac{1}{3}$ hours on Tuesday. How many hours has the team practiced so far this week?

The team has practiced _____ hours this week.

10.

11. There are $7\frac{1}{2}$ bottles of lemonade. Each bottle holds $1\frac{5}{6}$ quarts. How many quarts of lemonade are there?

There are _____ quarts of lemonade.

11.

Check What You Know

Decimals

Add, subtract, multiply, or divide.

	a	b	c	d
I.	$\begin{array}{r} 3.24 \\ +5.7 \\ \hline \end{array}$	$\begin{array}{r} 27.038 \\ +\ 0.725 \\ \hline \end{array}$	$\begin{array}{r} 3.21 \\ +6.034 \\ \hline \end{array}$	$\begin{array}{r} 7.2043 \\ 0.5817 \\ +1.35 \\ \hline \end{array}$
2.	$\begin{array}{r} 3.5 \\ -0.7 \\ \hline \end{array}$	$\begin{array}{r} 21.703 \\ -\ 8.6 \\ \hline \end{array}$	$\begin{array}{r} 17.015 \\ -\ 4.251 \\ \hline \end{array}$	$\begin{array}{r} 6.43 \\ -2.5167 \\ \hline \end{array}$
3.	$\begin{array}{r} 1.3 \\ \times 4.8 \\ \hline \end{array}$	$\begin{array}{r} 2.07 \\ \times\ 3.4 \\ \hline \end{array}$	$\begin{array}{r} 5.741 \\ \times\ 0.44 \\ \hline \end{array}$	$\begin{array}{r} 3.0162 \\ \times\ 2.9 \\ \hline \end{array}$
4.	$3\overline{)1.56}$	$7\overline{)2.135}$	$5\overline{)4.17}$	$2\overline{)6.8374}$
5.	$1.5\overline{)6}$	$.03\overline{)72}$	$1.75\overline{)67.55}$	$0.025\overline{)300}$
6.	$3.8\overline{)15.96}$	$0.14\overline{)0.4354}$	$5.25\overline{)45.15}$	$2.003\overline{)28.8432}$

Check What You Know

SHOW YOUR WORK

Decimals

Solve each problem.

7. A recipe calls for 1.75 cups of water, 0.5 cups of oil, and 0.2 cups of vinegar. What is the total amount of liquid in the recipe?

The recipe contains _____ cups of liquid.

7.

8. If a car averages 23.2 miles per gallon of gasoline, how far can it go on 15.25 gallons?

The car can go _____ miles.

8.

9. Todd's bill came to $37.68. He paid with $40.70. How much change should he get?

Todd should get _____ in change.

9.

10. Maria bought gifts for 7 of her friends. She spent $86.66. If she spent the same amount on each of her friends, how much did she spend on each?

Maria spent _____ on each friend.

10.

11. A small tree was measured at 3.67 feet tall. It can grow to 25 times that height. What is the tallest height the tree can be expected to reach?

The tree can reach _____ feet.

11.

12. It is 238.875 kilometers from Pikesville to Century Village. It is 422.75 kilometers from Pikesville to Fort Cedar. How much farther is it from Pikesville to Fort Cedar than from Pikesville to Century Village?

It is _____ kilometers farther to Fort Cedar.

12.

Lesson 3.1 Converting Decimals and Fractions

Convert $\frac{2}{5}$ to tenths.

$\frac{2}{5} = \frac{2 \times 2}{5 \times 2} = \frac{4}{10} = 0.4$

Convert $\frac{3}{20}$ to hundredths.

$\frac{3}{20} = \frac{3 \times 5}{20 \times 5} = \frac{15}{100} = 0.15$

Convert $\frac{12}{25}$ to thousandths.

$\frac{12}{25} = \frac{12 \times 40}{25 \times 40} = \frac{480}{1000} = 0.480$

Convert decimals to fractions or mixed numbers.

$0.6 = \frac{6}{10}$
$\quad = \frac{3}{5}$

$2.25 = 2\frac{25}{100}$
$\quad\quad = 2\frac{1}{4}$

$1.875 = 1\frac{875}{1000}$
$\quad\quad\quad = 1\frac{7}{8}$

Convert each fraction to a decimal.

	a	b	c
	Convert to tenths.	Convert to hundredths.	Convert to thousandths.
1.	$1\frac{3}{5}$ _____	$2\frac{1}{4}$ _____	$\frac{48}{200}$ _____
2.	$2\frac{1}{2}$ _____	$5\frac{6}{25}$ _____	$2\frac{23}{500}$ _____
3.	$5\frac{4}{5}$ _____	$1\frac{7}{20}$ _____	$6\frac{157}{250}$ _____
4.	$6\frac{1}{5}$ _____	$2\frac{9}{10}$ _____	$3\frac{72}{100}$ _____

Convert to ten thousandths.

5.	$3\frac{742}{1000}$ _____	$4\frac{56}{500}$ _____	$1\frac{1287}{2500}$ _____

Convert each decimal to a fraction or mixed numeral in simplest form.

6.	0.3 _____	1.6 _____	3.7 _____
7.	0.75 _____	5.86 _____	1.13 _____
8.	0.387 _____	2.588 _____	3.090 _____
9.	0.5329 _____	6.4273 _____	5.5825 _____

Lesson 3.2 Adding Decimals

When adding decimals, keep the decimal points aligned. Add as you would add whole numbers. It may be helpful to write in 0s as placeholders.

```
  | | | | |
  2 7 . 3 8 2 4              2 7 . 3 8 2 4
      1 . 4 3 7      OR          1 . 4 3 7 0  ←  The zero was added
  +   3 . 2 1 6 9             +   3 . 2 1 6 9       to mark place value.
  ─────────────              ─────────────
  3 2 . 0 3 6 3              3 2 . 0 3 6 3
```

Add.

	a	b	c	d	e
1.	$\begin{array}{r}0.7\\+0.4\\\hline\end{array}$	$\begin{array}{r}3.2\\+\ .8\\\hline\end{array}$	$\begin{array}{r}2.6\\+1.7\\\hline\end{array}$	$\begin{array}{r}5.1\\+2.6\\\hline\end{array}$	$\begin{array}{r}4.2\\+9.1\\\hline\end{array}$
2.	$\begin{array}{r}0.78\\+0.13\\\hline\end{array}$	$\begin{array}{r}1.07\\+2.38\\\hline\end{array}$	$\begin{array}{r}2.27\\+1.3\\\hline\end{array}$	$\begin{array}{r}6.58\\+1.04\\\hline\end{array}$	$\begin{array}{r}1.73\\+0.21\\\hline\end{array}$
3.	$\begin{array}{r}0.182\\+0.317\\\hline\end{array}$	$\begin{array}{r}1.077\\+3.25\\\hline\end{array}$	$\begin{array}{r}1.386\\+4.851\\\hline\end{array}$	$\begin{array}{r}2.01\\+3.503\\\hline\end{array}$	$\begin{array}{r}3.217\\+6.5\\\hline\end{array}$
4.	$\begin{array}{r}2.506\\+1.739\\\hline\end{array}$	$\begin{array}{r}0.38\\+1.934\\\hline\end{array}$	$\begin{array}{r}17.387\\+\ \ 5.04\\\hline\end{array}$	$\begin{array}{r}1.3426\\+2.5174\\\hline\end{array}$	$\begin{array}{r}6.2379\\+1.586\\\hline\end{array}$
5.	$\begin{array}{r}0.2837\\+5.421\\\hline\end{array}$	$\begin{array}{r}12.343\\+\ \ 1.6842\\\hline\end{array}$	$\begin{array}{r}38.256\\+27.181\\\hline\end{array}$	$\begin{array}{r}2.3\\+0.981\\\hline\end{array}$	$\begin{array}{r}5.632\\+1.7563\\\hline\end{array}$
6.	$\begin{array}{r}3.247\\0.18\\+1.511\\\hline\end{array}$	$\begin{array}{r}1.307\\2.1589\\+0.3707\\\hline\end{array}$	$\begin{array}{r}2.4168\\2.357\\+1.5623\\\hline\end{array}$	$\begin{array}{r}0.687\\1.03\\+5.7\\\hline\end{array}$	$\begin{array}{r}3.427\\1.0324\\+0.21\\\hline\end{array}$

Lesson 3.3   Subtracting Decimals

When subtracting decimals, keep the decimal points aligned. Subtract decimals as you would whole numbers. It may be helpful to write in 0s as placeholders.

$$
\begin{array}{r}
{\scriptstyle 2\ 15\ \ 10\ 11} \\
\cancel{3}\cancel{6}.\cancel{1}\,2 \\
-\ 7.386 \\
\hline
28.734
\end{array}
\quad \text{OR} \quad
\begin{array}{r}
{\scriptstyle 2\ 15\ \ 10\ 11\ 10} \\
\cancel{3}\cancel{6}.\cancel{1}\,2\,\cancel{0} \\
-\ 7.386 \\
\hline
28.734
\end{array}
$$

Subtract.

	a	b	c	d	e
1.	0.7 −0.2	1.38 −0.5	2.07 −1.13	3.821 −1.64	5.317 −2.436
2.	0.41 −0.25	0.247 −0.18	3.77 −2.09	4.396 −3.7	1.001 −0.2
3.	1.3 −1.186	2.791 −0.918	24.22 −3.653	3.028 −0.959	51.347 −12.018
4.	9.036 −0.741	24.03 −6.517	32 −5.56	8.9 −2.037	0.581 −0.3
5.	0.6 −0.427	3.413 −0.6	35.5 −6.28	2.7 −0.56	3.893 −1.2
6.	47 −0.593	6.824 −5.951	12.2 −9.58	21.03 −20.001	5.628 −0.07

Lesson 3.4   Problem Solving

Solve each problem.

1. Workers are using a piece of iron that is 0.324 millimeters thick and a piece of copper that is 0.671 millimeters thick. How much thicker is the copper?

The copper is _____ millimeters thicker.

2. Lenora bought a book for $12.36 and some school supplies for $7.29 and $5.47. How much did she spend?

She spent _____.

3. Joe's bill at the grocery store came to $6.08. He paid with a ten dollar bill and a dime. How much change did he get?

He received _____ in change.

4. One bottle holds 67.34 ounces and another bottle holds 48.5 ounces. Combined, how much do they hold?

The bottles hold _____ ounces combined.

5. A basic stereo system costs $189.67. An upgraded model costs $212.09. How much more does the upgraded model cost?

The upgraded model costs _____ more.

6. Lin ran 0.683 kilometers on Wednesday and 0.75 kilometers on Thursday. How far did he run on the two days combined?

He ran _____ kilometers over the two days.

7. A certain cabinet door is actually made of three thin boards that are pressed together. The boards are 0.371 inches, 0.13 inches, and 0.204 inches thick. How thick is the cabinet door?

The door is _____ inches thick.

1.

2.

3.

4.

5.

6.

7.

Lesson 3.5 Multiplying Decimals

When multiplying decimals, count the number of decimal places in each factor to figure out the placement of the decimal point in the product.

$$
\begin{array}{r} 3 \\ \times\ 5 \\ \hline 1\,5 \end{array}
$$
0 + 0 = 0
decimal places

$$
\begin{array}{r} 0.3 \\ \times\ \ \ 5 \\ \hline 1.5 \end{array}
$$
1 + 0 = 1
decimal place

$$
\begin{array}{r} 0.3 \\ \times 0.5 \\ \hline 0.15 \end{array}
$$
1 + 1 = 2
decimal places

$$
\begin{array}{r} 0.3 \\ \times 0.05 \\ \hline 0.015 \end{array}
$$
1 + 2 = 3
decimal places

Multiply.

	a	b	c	d	e
1.	1.2 × 3	0.61 × 4	0.58 × 12	1.212 × 3	32.7 × 2
2.	3.7 × 1.5	6.24 × 2.8	3.73 × 0.77	4.389 × 0.6	1.7924 × 2.5
3.	5.06 × 1.1	7.301 × 0.2	3.46 × 8.7	0.571 × 9	1.6342 × 2.7
4.	6.07 × 3	5.826 × 0.4	2.103 × 1.01	4.35 × 0.8	7.4213 × 6

Lesson 3.6   Dividing Decimals by Whole Numbers

When dividing a decimal by any whole number, place the decimal point in the quotient directly above the decimal point in the dividend.

```
      5.4              0.54             .054              .0054
 6)32.4           6)3.24           6)0.324           6)0.0324
  -30              -30              -30               -30
    24               24               24                24
  -24              -24              -24               -24
    0                0                0                 0
```

Divide.

	a	b	c	d
1.	4)0.48	2)7.6	5)1.75	3)9.03
2.	9)8.181	7)2.877	3)15.024	2)1.3548
3.	3)0.0096	2)1.54	4)3.228	5)2.570
4.	6)0.696	8)7.216	9)0.1899	7)7.6349

Lesson 3.7 Dividing Whole Numbers by Decimals

Multiply the divisor and dividend by 10, 100, or 1000 so the new divisor is a whole number.

$$0.7\overline{)49} = 7\overline{)490} \quad \begin{array}{r} 70 \\ -490 \\ \hline 0 \end{array}$$

$$.06\overline{)24} = 6\overline{)2400} \quad \begin{array}{r} 400 \\ -2400 \\ \hline 0 \end{array}$$

$$.005\overline{)3} = 5\overline{)3000} \quad \begin{array}{r} 600 \\ -3000 \\ \hline 0 \end{array}$$

Divide.

	a	b	c	d
1.	$0.3\overline{)42}$	$0.5\overline{)25}$	$0.04\overline{)24}$	$0.06\overline{)6}$
2.	$3.3\overline{)99}$	$2.5\overline{)10}$	$0.18\overline{)72}$	$0.009\overline{)63}$
3.	$1.2\overline{)6}$	$0.21\overline{)42}$	$0.05\overline{)75}$	$0.025\overline{)50}$
4.	$0.7\overline{)84}$	$0.08\overline{)128}$	$0.003\overline{)132}$	$0.002\overline{)344}$

Lesson 3.8 Dividing Decimals by Decimals

Multiply the divisor and the dividend by the same power of 10 to change the divisor to a whole number.

$$
1.5 \overline{)40.5} = 15 \overline{)405} \\
\begin{array}{r} 27 \\ -30 \\ \hline 105 \\ -105 \\ \hline 0 \end{array}
$$

$$
1.05 \overline{)2.415} = 105 \overline{)241.5} \\
\begin{array}{r} 2.3 \\ -210 \\ \hline 315 \\ -315 \\ \hline 0 \end{array}
$$

Divide.

	a	b	c	d
1.	$0.03 \overline{)45.6}$	$1.7 \overline{)20.4}$	$3.8 \overline{)16.72}$	$0.5 \overline{)1.875}$
2.	$7.4 \overline{)28.86}$	$1.07 \overline{)67.41}$	$0.22 \overline{)8.03}$	$0.15 \overline{)0.9423}$
3.	$0.08 \overline{)2.524}$	$0.027 \overline{)6.561}$	$1.5 \overline{)9.5025}$	$6.4 \overline{)27.04}$
4.	$0.95 \overline{)0.6175}$	$0.008 \overline{)0.1736}$	$0.175 \overline{)3.0625}$	$2.388 \overline{)3.3432}$

Lesson 3.9 Multiplication and Division Practice

Multiply or divide.

	a	**b**	**c**	**d**
1.	0.2 × 1.3	4.37 × 2.6	3.771 × 0.5	1.3794 × 4.6
2.	8.7 × 6.2	0.301 × 1.02	5.007 × 2.8	0.2109 × 3.4

3. $3\overline{)0.36}$ $5\overline{)4.55}$ $7\overline{)0.63}$ $8\overline{)0.048}$

4. $7\overline{)14.42}$ $9\overline{)36.081}$ $2\overline{)5.422}$ $6\overline{)3.6090}$

5. $0.5\overline{)45}$ $1.3\overline{)39}$ $3.6\overline{)324}$ $0.04\overline{)12}$

6. $0.15\overline{)5.4}$ $8.01\overline{)10.413}$ $2.9\overline{)98.02}$ $0.08\overline{)1.896}$

7. $0.0009\overline{)54}$ $2.01\overline{)7.638}$ $4.17\overline{)10.6335}$ $1.003\overline{)37.111}$

Lesson 3.10   Problem Solving

SHOW YOUR WORK

Solve each problem.

1. Fred bought 7 games on clearance for $104.65. Each game was on sale for the same price. How much did each game cost?

   Each game cost _____.

2. Gas costs $1.64 a gallon. Elaine spent $23.78 at the gas station. How many gallons of gas did she buy?

   Elaine bought _____ gallons of gas.

3. There are 2.5 servings in a can of tuna fish. How many servings are there in 7 cans?

   There are _____ servings in 7 cans.

4. A grain distributor can process 14.6 tons of grain an hour. How much can the distributor process in 8.75 hours?

   The distributor can process _____ tons of grain.

5. Rhonda earned $324.65 delivering newspapers. She promised her sister 0.2 of her earnings for helping her. How much does Rhonda owe her sister?

   Rhonda owes her sister _____.

6. A car traveled 48.36 miles in one hour. What was its average speed per minute?

   Its average speed was _____ miles per minute.

7. There are 5.28 cups of pudding to be put into 6 dishes. How much pudding should be put into each dish to make them equal?

   Each dish should get _____ cups of pudding.

1.

2.

3.

4.

5.

6.

7.

Check What You Learned

Decimals

Add, subtract, multiply, or divide.

	a	b	c	d
1.	0.23 +0.9	78.07 + 1.34	9.065 +2.78	48.761 + 9.0374
2.	1.379 6.04 +3.4173	28.46 3.7748 + 0.011	5.8 −2.9	33.04 − 6.75
3.	29.083 − 2.1	13.732 − 8.64	3.89 −1.476	8.201 −3.9376
4.	6.2 ×0.4	3.05 ×2.83	5.736 × 8.2	4.0327 × 1.1

5. 7)9.52   2)3.586   0.25)65   0.04)19

6. 0.7)13.237   3.8)22.8   7.3)2.847   3.107)43.1873

Check What You Learned

Decimals

Solve each problem.

7. Sheila bought three books for $12.63, $9.05, and $14.97. How much did she spend?

   Sheila spent _____ on the three books.

   7.

8. Roberto bought a 12-pack of bottled water. Each bottle held 0.75 liters. How many liters of water did he buy?

   Roberto bought _____ liters.

   8.

9. The highest batting average on the Owls baseball team is 0.427. The lowest batting average is 0.189. What is the difference?

   The difference is _____.

   9.

10. Lou spent $17.65 to buy 5 items of equal value. How much did he spend on each?

    Lou spent _____ on each item.

    10.

11. A hike is 26.4 miles. Alicia wants to divide it equally over 3 days. How far does she need to hike each day?

    She needs to hike _____ miles each day.

    11.

12. There are 6.75 buckets of sand in a sandbox. If each full bucket holds 4.32 pounds of sand, how many pounds of sand are there in the sandbox?

    There are _____ pounds of sand in the sandbox.

    12.

Check What You Know

Finding Percents

Change each of the following to percents.

	a	b	c
1.	$\frac{41}{50}$ = _____ %	$\frac{7}{20}$ = _____ %	$\frac{3}{5}$ = _____ %
2.	3.5 = _____ %	7.25 = _____ %	0.3 = _____ %

Change each of the following to decimals.

3.	20% = _____	38% = _____	127% = _____
4.	$12\frac{1}{2}$% = _____	$7\frac{3}{5}$% = _____	$22\frac{1}{4}$% = _____

Change each of the following to fractions in simplest form.

5.	25% = _____	40% = _____	320% = _____

Complete the following.

6. _____ is 8% of 20.   _____ is 25% of 56.   _____ is 40% of 6.

7. _____ is 110% of 90.   _____ is 2% of 2.   _____ is 75% of 80.

8. 8 is 25% of _____.   25 is 12.5% of _____.   70 is 200% of _____.

9. 3.5 is 20% of _____.   0.2 is 5% of _____.   1.65 is $5\frac{1}{2}$% of _____.

10. 100 is _____% of 400.   0.4 is _____% of 0.5.   74 is _____% of 37.

11. 9 is _____% of 60.   12 is _____% of 600.   23 is _____% of 115.

NAME _____

Check What You Know

Finding Percents

Solve each problem.

12. A grocery store is offering a 2% savings if customers bag their own groceries. How much will Akira save on a purchase of $215.50?

He will save _____.

13.

13. A home improvement company gives a 30% discount for all projects over $1,000. If the original cost of Praveen's project is $2,545, how much will he save with the discount?

He will save _____.

13.

14. A restaurant charges an automatic 20% tip for groups of 6 or more. A group of 8 people had a bill of $187. How much was their tip?

Their tip was _____.

14.

15. A department store has a policy of charging a 15% service charge on all returned checks. If a check for $725 is returned, how much will the service charge be?

The service charge will be _____.

15.

16. A mail order company charges $4\frac{1}{2}$% for shipping and handling on all orders. How much is the shipping and handling charge on an order of $52?

The shipping charge is _____.

16.

17. The phone company charges a 1.5% service fee on all long distance calls. If a long distance bill is $32, how much is the service fee?

The service fee is _____.

17.

Lesson 4.1   Understanding Percents

Percent means how many out of 100 and is expressed with the symbol **%**. Percents can also be expressed as fractions with a denominator of 100 and as decimals.

$$25\% = \frac{25}{100} = \frac{1}{4} \text{ or } 0.25 \qquad\qquad 9\% = \frac{9}{100} \text{ or } 0.09$$

Complete the following. Write fractions in simplest form.

	Percent	**Fraction**	**Decimal**
1.	7%	_____	_____
2.	13%	_____	_____
3.	48%	_____	_____
4.	71%	_____	_____
5.	27%	_____	_____
6.	2%	_____	_____
7.	15%	_____	_____
8.	39%	_____	_____
9.	10%	_____	_____
10.	62%	_____	_____
11.	75%	_____	_____
12.	97%	_____	_____
13.	53%	_____	_____
14.	82%	_____	_____

Lesson 4.2 Comparing Percents, Fractions, and Decimals

Use inequality symbols to compare percents, fractions, and decimals.

Express the numbers in the same format so they are easier to compare.

Symbol	Meaning
>	greater than
<	less than
=	equal to

$\frac{1}{5}$ _____ 30%   0.45 _____ 38%

20% _____ 30%   Convert 1 of the numbers.   45% _____ 38%

20% __<__ 30%   Compare the numbers   45% __>__ 38%

Write >, <, or = on the line to compare the given quantities.

	a	**b**	**c**
1.	13% _____ $\frac{2}{5}$	0.35 _____ $\frac{1}{8}$	$\frac{1}{4}$ _____ 0.25
2.	87% _____ 0.79	18 _____ 18%	$\frac{1}{2}$ _____ 0.42
3.	$\frac{9}{10}$ _____ 9%	40% _____ $\frac{4}{5}$	0.72 _____ $\frac{2}{3}$
4.	0.82 _____ $\frac{41}{50}$	63% _____ $\frac{1}{2}$	14% _____ 0.014
5.	$\frac{1}{3}$ _____ 50%	$\frac{4}{5}$ _____ 80%	0.07 _____ $\frac{1}{10}$
6.	$\frac{250}{100}$ _____ 2.5	0.25 _____ $\frac{1}{3}$	318 _____ 3.18%
7.	50% _____ $\frac{2}{3}$	93% _____ 0.93	22% _____ $\frac{1}{4}$
8.	0.67 _____ $\frac{3}{5}$	$\frac{1}{2}$ _____ 20%	642% _____ 6.42
9.	0.08 _____ 80%	50% _____ $\frac{3}{4}$	$\frac{1}{2}$ _____ 0.050
10.	$\frac{2}{5}$ _____ 2.5	70% _____ $\frac{7}{10}$	$\frac{147}{100}$ _____ 14%
11.	$\frac{45}{100}$ _____ 55%	1238% _____ 12.38	$16\frac{2}{5}$ _____ 16.25
12.	3.75 _____ 375%	0.15 _____ $\frac{1}{5}$	7.5 _____ $\frac{3}{4}$
13.	$\frac{13}{25}$ _____ 49%	0.45 _____ $\frac{7}{20}$	3% _____ 0.03
14.	25% _____ $\frac{11}{50}$	$12\frac{1}{5}$ _____ 12.2	18% _____ $\frac{1}{4}$

Lesson 4.3 Ordering Percents, Fractions, and Decimals

To put percents, fractions, and decimals in a certain order, first write the numbers in the same format so they are easier to compare. Compare and order the numbers. Then, rewrite the numbers in their original forms.

Order 25%, $\frac{2}{3}$, $\frac{4}{5}$, and 0.37 from greatest to least.

Rewrite: 0.25, 0.67, 0.8, 0.37

Order: 0.8, 0.67, 0.37, 0.25

Rewrite: $\frac{4}{5}$, $\frac{2}{3}$, 0.37, 25%

Order from least to greatest.

	a	**b**
1.	13%, $\frac{1}{3}$, 0.35, $\frac{1}{4}$	$\frac{3}{4}$, 72%, 0.02, 0.34
2.	$\frac{2}{5}$, 45%, 0.25, $\frac{1}{3}$	$\frac{1}{10}$, 1%, $\frac{11}{100}$, 0.15
3.	143%, 14.5, $\frac{14}{25}$, $\frac{14}{100}$	68%, 0.55, $\frac{3}{5}$, 0.63

Order from greatest to least.

	a	**b**
4.	$3\frac{1}{2}$, 35%, 320%, $\frac{3}{100}$	$\frac{1}{4}$, $\frac{1}{5}$, 0.4, 0.5, 30%
5.	0.625, $\frac{7}{8}$, 60%, $\frac{3}{4}$	17%, $\frac{1}{7}$, 1.7, 0.017
6.	406%, 4.1, $\frac{40}{100}$, $\frac{4}{5}$	$\frac{16}{5}$, $5\frac{2}{5}$, 32%, 16%

Lesson 4.4　Percent to Fraction and Fraction to Percent

Multiply by $\frac{1}{100}$ to change a percent to a fraction or mixed numeral in simplest form.

$$120\% = 120 \times \frac{1}{100}$$
$$= \frac{120}{100}$$
$$= \frac{6}{5} = 1\frac{1}{5}$$

Multiply by a factor of 100 to change a fraction or mixed numeral to a percent.

$$2\frac{3}{5} = \frac{13}{5} \times \frac{20}{20} = \frac{260}{100}$$
$$= 260 \times \frac{1}{100}$$
$$= 260\%$$

Change fractions and mixed numerals to percents. Change percents to fractions or mixed numerals in simplest form.

	a	b	c	d
1.	75% = _____	$\frac{7}{25}$ = _____ %	$\frac{16}{50}$ = _____ %	98% = _____
2.	56% = _____	48% = _____	$2\frac{2}{5}$ = _____ %	$9\frac{3}{10}$ = _____ %
3.	$\frac{31}{50}$ = _____ %	$\frac{9}{20}$ = _____ %	12% = _____	425% = _____
4.	$7\frac{3}{5}$ = _____ %	15% = _____	$2\frac{1}{4}$ = _____ %	31% = _____
5.	60% = _____	$\frac{1}{5}$ = _____ %	$\frac{1}{2}$ = _____ %	72% = _____
6.	$3\frac{3}{4}$ = _____ %	135% = _____	40% = _____	$\frac{14}{25}$ = _____ %
7.	$\frac{17}{20}$ = _____ %	$\frac{5}{8}$ = _____ %	65% = _____	10% = _____
8.	5% = _____	$10\frac{4}{25}$ = _____ %	50% = _____	$3\frac{7}{20}$ = _____ %

Lesson 4.5 Percent to Decimal and Decimal to Percent

Study how a percent is changed to a decimal and a decimal is changed to a percent.

$$6.75\% = 6.75 \times 0.01$$
$$= 0.0675$$

$$1.35 = \frac{135}{100}$$
$$= 135\%$$

Change each of the following percents to decimals and decimals to percents.

	a	b	c
1.	85% = _____	1.47 = _____%	17% = _____
2.	0.38 = _____%	8.32% = _____	0.69 = _____%
3.	27% = _____	0.05 = _____%	2.1% = _____
4.	1.50 = _____%	15% = _____	0.426 = _____%
5.	33.5% = _____	0.65 = _____%	9.25% = _____
6.	0.039 = _____%	52.6% = _____	4.85 = _____%
7.	5.5% = _____	0.225 = _____%	6.25% = _____
8.	0.005 = _____%	525% = _____	0.7 = _____%
9.	0.1% = _____	0.1 = _____%	63.2% = _____

Lesson 4.5 Percent to Decimal and Decimal to Percent

If a percent is expressed as a fraction, first change that fraction to a decimal.
Then, change the percent to a decimal.

$$2\tfrac{1}{2}\% = 2.5\% = 2.5 \times 0.01 = 0.025$$

Change each of the following to decimals.

	a	b	c
1.	$25\tfrac{1}{4}\% =$ _____	$3\tfrac{1}{2}\% =$ _____	$2\tfrac{7}{10}\% =$ _____
2.	$15\tfrac{1}{20}\% =$ _____	$63\tfrac{1}{5}\% =$ _____	$12\tfrac{17}{25}\% =$ _____
3.	$5\tfrac{3}{4}\% =$ _____	$11\tfrac{3}{10}\% =$ _____	$42\tfrac{3}{4}\% =$ _____
4.	$17\tfrac{1}{2}\% =$ _____	$22\tfrac{2}{5}\% =$ _____	$75\tfrac{9}{20}\% =$ _____
5.	$9\tfrac{3}{5}\% =$ _____	$18\tfrac{2}{25}\% =$ _____	$52\tfrac{1}{4}\% =$ _____
6.	$3\tfrac{19}{50}\% =$ _____	$39\tfrac{1}{10}\% =$ _____	$83\tfrac{12}{25}\% =$ _____
7.	$15\tfrac{1}{5}\% =$ _____	$79\tfrac{4}{25}\% =$ _____	$27\tfrac{3}{4}\% =$ _____
8.	$38\tfrac{19}{20}\% =$ _____	$8\tfrac{9}{10}\% =$ _____	$93\tfrac{18}{25}\% =$ _____
9.	$48\tfrac{33}{50}\% =$ _____	$3\tfrac{2}{5}\% =$ _____	$81\tfrac{7}{10}\% =$ _____
10.	$50\tfrac{1}{2}\% =$ _____	$14\tfrac{1}{2}\% =$ _____	$45\tfrac{3}{4}\% =$ _____

Lesson 4.6 Finding the Percent of a Number

To find a percent of a number, express the percent as a fraction or a decimal and multiply.

_____ = 20% of 65	_____ = 20% of 65
_____ = $\frac{1}{5} \times 65$	_____ = 0.2 × 65
_____ = $\frac{65}{5}$ = 13	_____ = 13
13 is 20% of 65.	13 is 20% of 65.

Complete the following.

	a	b	c
1.	_____ is 25% of 50.	_____ is 30% of 65.	_____ is 50% of 38.5.
2.	_____ is 20% of 73.	_____ is 5% of 32.	_____ is 12% of 47.
3.	_____ is 25% of 14.	_____ is 45% of 93.	_____ is $6\frac{1}{4}$% of 30.
4.	_____ is 52% of 6.	_____ is $5\frac{1}{2}$% of 16.	_____ is 20% of 412.
5.	_____ is $7\frac{3}{4}$% of 16.	_____ is 10% of 3.6.	_____ is 49% of 7.8.
6.	_____ is 3% of 98.	_____ is 15% of 23.2.	_____ is 75% of 45.
7.	_____ is 5% of 3.	_____ is 30% of 11.	_____ is 40% of 126.
8.	_____ is $2\frac{1}{2}$% of 320.	_____ is 95% of 125.	_____ is 80% of 60.
9.	_____ is 4% of 20.	_____ is $9\frac{1}{2}$% of 109.	_____ is 55% of 95.
10.	_____ is 45% of 105.	_____ is 70% of 565.	_____ is 35% of 7.

Lesson 4.6   Finding the Percent of a Number

11.7 is what percent of 65?

$11.7 = n\% \times 65$	Write the expression as a sentence.
$11.7 = \frac{n}{100} \times \frac{65}{1}$	Express the percent as a fraction.
$\frac{11.7}{1} = \frac{n \times 65}{100}$	Rewrite both sides as fractions.
$1170 = n \times 65$	Multiply both sides by 100.
$\frac{1170}{65} = n$	Divide both sides by 65.
$18 = n$	11.7 is ___18%___ of 65.

Complete the following.

	a	b	c
1.	12 is _____% of 48.	75 is _____% of 300.	37 is _____% of 74.
2.	7.2 is _____% of 30.	160 is _____% of 80.	60 is _____% of 40.
3.	3 is _____% of 20.	7 is _____% of 5.	27.9 is _____% of 93.
4.	28.8 is _____% of 72.	11.25 is _____% of 15.	29.6 is _____% of 37.
5.	17.25 is _____% of 100.	16 is _____% of 80.	6.25 is _____% of 125.
6.	5 is _____% of 25.	5 is _____% of 50.	5 is _____% of 100.
7.	4 is _____% of 400.	4.5 is _____% of 60.	11 is _____% of 20.
8.	11.25 is _____% of 90.	10 is _____% of 40.	50 is _____% of 80.
9.	76.5 is _____% of 90.	25 is _____% of 500.	72 is _____% of 60.
10.	250 is _____% of 50.	100 is _____% of 800.	16.5 is _____% of 16.5.

Lesson 4.6   Finding the Percent of a Number

17 is 25% of what number?

17	$= 25\% \times n$		Write the question as a number sentence.

$\frac{17}{1} = \frac{25}{100} \times \frac{n}{1}$ OR $17 = 0.25 \times n$ Express as fraction or decimal.

$1700 = 25 \times n$ Multiply.

$\frac{1700}{25} = n$ $\frac{17}{0.25} = \frac{0.25 \times n}{0.25}$ Divide.

$68 = n$ $68 = n$ 17 is 25% of $\underline{68}$.

Complete the following.

	a	b	c
1.	32 is 50% of _____.	7 is 20% of _____.	15 is 12% of _____.
2.	5 is 200% of _____.	83 is 25% of _____.	10 is 25% of _____.
3.	75 is 25% of _____.	12 is 80% of _____.	4.5 is 9% of _____.
4.	7.25 is 2.5% of _____.	80 is 40% of _____.	35 is 70% of _____.
5.	3.86 is 20% of _____.	0.3 is 60% of _____.	8 is 8% of _____.
6.	33 is 66% of _____.	5.25 is 35% of _____.	6.25 is 25% of _____.
7.	15.75 is 35% of _____.	17.16 is 22% of _____.	78.85 is 83% of _____.
8.	55.2 is 120% of _____.	1.12 is 2% of _____.	71 is 71% of _____.
9.	100 is 20% of _____.	146 is 200% of _____.	0.8 is 40% of _____.
10.	75.24 is 22% of _____.	1.5 is 10% of _____.	11 is 55% of _____.

Lesson 4.7 Problem Solving

SHOW YOUR WORK

Solve each problem.

1. Mika's lunch came to $12.50. She wants to leave an
   18% tip. How much should she leave?

   She should leave a _____ tip.

   1.

2. A store is having a 25%-off sale. If an item originally
   cost $19.36, how much should be taken off the price?

   _____ should be taken off the original price.

   2.

3. Dario bought a new bike for $90.00. Sales tax is $5\frac{1}{2}$%.
   How much tax does he have to pay? How much is his
   total bill?

   Dario's tax is _____.

   Dario's total bill is _____.

   3.

4. Tai used a coupon and bought a sweater for $32. The
   full retail price of the sweater was $40. What percent
   did Tai save with her coupon?

   Tai saved _____% with her coupon.

   4.

5. Owen made a down payment of $1,600 on a car. That
   was 20% of the total price. What was the total price of
   the car?

   The total price of the car was _____.

   5.

6. A store allows customers to buy 3 items of the same
   price and get 2 more of the same items free. What
   percent savings does this represent?

   This represents a _____% savings.

   6.

Check What You Learned

Finding Percents

Change each of the following to percents.

a	b	c
1. $\frac{2}{5}$ = _____ %	$\frac{9}{10}$ = _____ %	$\frac{3}{20}$ = _____ %
2. 0.42 = _____ %	1.3 = _____ %	0.01 = _____ %

Change each of the following to decimals.

3. 53% = _____   250% = _____   8% = _____

4. $7\frac{3}{4}$% = _____ $29\frac{1}{5}$% = _____ $5\frac{1}{10}$% = _____

Change each of the following to fractions in simplest form.

5. 475% = _____   60% = _____   155% = _____

Complete the following.

6. _____ is 20% of 10.   _____ is 5% of 76.   _____ is 60% of 120.

7. _____ is 140% of 80.   _____ is 75% of 0.4.   _____ is 10% of 0.08.

8. 95 is _____% of 23.75.   60 is _____% of 80.   45 is _____% of 300.

9. 0.15 is _____% of 30.   33 is _____% of 110.   63 is _____% of 126.

10. 11 is 80% of _____.   0.5 is 10% of _____.   24 is 300% of _____.

11. 8 is 40% of _____.   45 is 4.5% of _____.   123.75 is 75% of _____.

Check What You Learned

Finding Percents

Solve each problem.

12. A store is offering a special on CDs. If a customer buys four CDs at the regular price, the fifth one is 25% off. If the regular price is $16.76, how much will the customer save on the fifth CD?

The customer will save _____.

12.

13. Vito bought a book that retails for $23.80. He used a coupon for 15% off. How much money did he save?

Vito saved _____.

13.

14. Diana bought some art supplies. The total came to $38.00, plus tax. There is a $6\frac{1}{2}$% sales tax. How much tax did she pay?

Diana paid _____ in tax.

14.

15. Pete wants to buy a car for $8,200. Pete has to make a down payment of $1,640. What percent of the car's total price is that?

The down payment is _____% of the car's total price.

15.

16. Danielle bought a gift for a friend that originally cost $32. She used a coupon to get $5 off. What percent did she save?

Danielle saved _____%.

16.

17. Ines is saving to buy some computer equipment that costs $690. Her parents have offered to pay for 45% of the equipment. How much money does Ines need to save?

Ines needs to save _____.

17.

Check What You Know

Calculating Interest

Complete the following.

	Principal	Rate	Time	Interest	Total Amount
1.	$525	6%	1 year	_____	_____
2.	$380	8%	1 year	_____	_____
3.	$714	12%	1 year	_____	_____
4.	$1,250	7%	1 year	_____	_____
5.	$500	9%	3 years	_____	_____
6.	$650	$3\frac{1}{4}$%	4 years	_____	_____
7.	$820	$5\frac{1}{2}$%	2 years	_____	_____
8.	$300	$7\frac{3}{4}$%	6 years	_____	_____
9.	$1,000	$2\frac{1}{4}$%	$1\frac{1}{2}$ years	_____	_____
10.	$520	$3\frac{1}{2}$%	$2\frac{3}{4}$ years	_____	_____
11.	$4,200	6%	$5\frac{1}{4}$ years	_____	_____
12.	$1,700	$4\frac{1}{2}$%	$3\frac{1}{2}$ years	_____	_____
13.	$50	8%	$\frac{1}{2}$ year	_____	_____
14.	$1,400	$12\frac{1}{2}$%	$\frac{3}{4}$ year	_____	_____
15.	$280	$6\frac{1}{2}$%	$\frac{1}{4}$ year	_____	_____

NAME _____

Check What You Know

SHOW YOUR WORK

Calculating Interest

Solve each problem.

16. Sarah has $480 in her savings account earning $4\frac{1}{4}$% interest. How much interest will she earn in $2\frac{1}{2}$ years? How much money will be in the account after $2\frac{1}{2}$ years?

Sara will earn _____ in interest in $2\frac{1}{2}$ years.

After $2\frac{1}{2}$ years, _____ will be in Sarah's account.

16.

17. The Turners borrowed $20,000 to invest in a new business. The loan is for 15 years at $5\frac{1}{4}$% interest. How much interest will they pay? How much will their total payments be?

The Turners will pay _____ in interest.

Their total payments will be _____.

17.

18. Bianca borrowed $120 for 9 months ($\frac{3}{4}$ year) at $3\frac{1}{2}$% interest. How much interest will she pay? What is the total amount she will pay back?

Bianca will pay _____ in interest.

The total amount she will pay back is _____.

18.

19. Ed bought a $50 bond that pays $8\frac{1}{4}$% interest. It comes due in 2 years. How much interest will he get? How much will the bond be worth?

Ed will get _____ in interest.

The bond will be worth _____.

19.

20. A store allows customers 1 year to pay for their purchases, but it charges 14% interest. How much interest would be charged on a purchase of $620? What is the total amount the customer would pay?

The interest would be _____.

The customer would pay a total amount of _____.

20.

Lesson 5.1 Simple Interest for One Year

Simple interest is determined by multiplying the amount of money (principal, or *p*) by the rate of interest (*r*) by the number of years (time, or *t*). This can be written as $I = prt$.

What is the simple interest on $400 deposited in a savings account paying 3% for 1 year?

$I = prt$

$I = 400 \times 0.03 \times 1$

$I = \$12.00$

Complete the following.

	Principal	Rate	Time	Interest
1.	$650	3%	1 year	_____
2.	$700	2%	1 year	_____
3.	$400	4%	1 year	_____
4.	$175	5%	1 year	_____
5.	$250	7%	1 year	_____
6.	$325	6%	1 year	_____
7.	$415	4%	1 year	_____
8.	$318.80	5%	1 year	_____
9.	$725	3%	1 year	_____
10.	$850	7%	1 year	_____
11.	$575	8%	1 year	_____
12.	$925	5%	1 year	_____
13.	$545.50	4%	1 year	_____
14.	$1,380	7%	1 year	_____

Lesson 5.1   Problem Solving

Solve each problem.

1. Mr. Johnson borrowed $750 for 1 year. He has to pay
    6% simple interest. How much interest will he pay?

    Mr. Johnson will pay _____ in interest.

2. Mrs. Soto invested in a certificate of deposit that pays
    8% interest. Her investment was $325. How much
    interest will she receive in 1 year?

    Mrs. Soto will receive _____ in interest.

3. Andrea put $52 in a savings account that pays 4%
    interest. How much interest will she earn in 1 year?

    Andrea will earn _____ in interest.

4. Ms. Wilson took out a $1,500 loan. The interest rate is
    7%. How much interest will she pay in 1 year?

    Ms. Wilson will pay _____ in interest.

5. Mr. Perez loaned $450 to his son for 1 year at 2%
    interest. How much interest will he collect?

    Mr. Perez will collect _____ in interest.

6. Jackson's savings account contains $827.50. If the
    interest rate is 4%, how much interest will the money
    earn in 1 year?

    The money will earn _____.

7. A special bond is being issued. It pays 13% for
    investments of $2,500. How much interest will it pay
    in 1 year?

    The bond will pay _____ in interest.

1.
2.
3.
4.
5.
6.
7.

Lesson 5.2 Simple Interest for More Than One Year

What is the simple interest on $700 deposited in a savings account for 4 years paying $5\frac{1}{4}$% interest? How much money will be in the account at the end of 4 years?

$$I = p \times r \times t = 700 \times 0.0525 \times 4$$
$$= 147$$
$$\text{Total} = I + p = 147 + 700 = \$847 \text{ in the account.}$$

Complete the following.

	Principal	Rate	Time	Interest	Total Amount
1.	$500	$10\frac{1}{2}$%	2 years	_____	_____
2.	$750	8%	3 years	_____	_____
3.	$425	$9\frac{1}{2}$%	4 years	_____	_____
4.	$600	$4\frac{1}{4}$%	6 years	_____	_____
5.	$350	12%	4 years	_____	_____
6.	$700	$3\frac{1}{2}$%	3 years	_____	_____
7.	$850	7%	7 years	_____	_____
8.	$1,025	$5\frac{1}{2}$%	4 years	_____	_____
9.	$800	$4\frac{3}{4}$%	5 years	_____	_____
10.	$1,500	$6\frac{1}{2}$%	2 years	_____	_____
11.	$2,250	5%	3 years	_____	_____
12.	$1,385	$2\frac{1}{2}$%	6 years	_____	_____

Lesson 5.2   Simple Interest for More Than One Year

What is the simple interest on $800 deposited in a savings account for $3\frac{1}{2}$ years paying 4% interest? How much money will be in the account at the end of $3\frac{1}{2}$ years?

$$I = p \times r \times t = 800 \times 0.04 \times 3.5$$
$$= 112$$
$$I + p = 112 + 800 = \$912 \text{ in the account.}$$

Complete the following.

	Principal	Rate	Time	Interest	Total Amount
1.	$500	$5\frac{1}{2}$%	$3\frac{1}{2}$ years	_____	_____
2.	$180	10%	$1\frac{3}{4}$ years	_____	_____
3.	$720	$6\frac{1}{2}$%	$2\frac{1}{4}$ years	_____	_____
4.	$650	$4\frac{1}{4}$%	4 years	_____	_____
5.	$585	8%	$5\frac{1}{2}$ years	_____	_____
6.	$1,600	$9\frac{1}{4}$%	$2\frac{1}{2}$ years	_____	_____
7.	$60	$2\frac{1}{2}$%	$3\frac{1}{2}$ years	_____	_____
8.	$700	6%	$3\frac{1}{4}$ years	_____	_____
9.	$2,200	$5\frac{1}{4}$%	$4\frac{1}{2}$ years	_____	_____
10.	$1,350	7%	$6\frac{1}{2}$ years	_____	_____
11.	$400	12%	$5\frac{3}{4}$ years	_____	_____
12.	$5,000	18%	$6\frac{3}{4}$ years	_____	_____

Lesson 5.3 Simple Interest for Less Than One Year

What is the simple interest on a $500 loan at $6\frac{1}{2}$% interest for $\frac{1}{2}$ year? How much total will be paid back?

$$I = p \times r \times t = 500 \times 0.065 \times 0.5$$
$$= 16.25$$
$$I + p = 16.25 + 500 = \$516.25 \text{ to be paid.}$$

Complete the following.

	Principal	Rate	Time	Interest	Total Amount
1.	$700	6%	$\frac{3}{4}$ year	_____	_____
2.	$500	$4\frac{1}{2}$%	$\frac{1}{2}$ year	_____	_____
3.	$850	8%	$\frac{1}{4}$ year	_____	_____
4.	$1,200	$6\frac{1}{2}$%	$\frac{1}{4}$ year	_____	_____
5.	$425	4%	$\frac{3}{4}$ year	_____	_____
6.	$200	18%	$\frac{1}{2}$ year	_____	_____
7.	$2,500	7%	$\frac{3}{4}$ year	_____	_____
8.	$3,000	$5\frac{1}{2}$%	$\frac{1}{4}$ year	_____	_____
9.	$50	3%	$\frac{1}{2}$ year	_____	_____
10.	$720	11%	$\frac{3}{4}$ year	_____	_____

Lesson 5.3 Problem Solving

Solve each problem.

1. Crystal borrowed $500 for $\frac{1}{4}$ year at 8% interest. How much interest did the bank charge? How much total did she pay at the end of the term?

   The bank charged _____ in interest.

   Crystal paid _____ total.

2. Drew invested $360 for $2\frac{1}{2}$ years at $7\frac{1}{4}$% interest. How much interest did he earn? How much money did he have after $2\frac{1}{2}$ years?

   Drew earned _____ in interest.

   Drew had a total of _____ after $2\frac{1}{2}$ years.

3. Jonas purchased a 42-month ($3\frac{1}{2}$ year) certificate of deposit. It cost $600 and pays 7% interest. How much interest will he get? How much will the certificate be worth when he cashes it in?

   Jonas will get _____ in interest.

   The certificate will be worth _____.

4. Rick borrowed $50 from his sister for 3 months ($\frac{1}{4}$ year). She charged him 14% interest. How much does Rick have to pay to his sister?

   Rick must pay his sister a total of _____.

5. The grocery store borrowed $15,000 to remodel. The term is 7 years and the interest rate is $4\frac{1}{4}$%. How much interest will the store pay? What is the total amount to be repaid?

   The store will pay _____ in interest.

   The total amount to be repaid is _____.

1.

2.

3.

4.

5.

Check What You Learned

Calculating Interest

Complete the following.

	Principal	Rate	Time	Interest	Total Amount
1.	$450	8%	1 year	_____	_____
2.	$630	5%	1 year	_____	_____
3.	$275	4%	1 year	_____	_____
4.	$595.50	6%	1 year	_____	_____
5.	$360	$5\frac{1}{2}$%	2 years	_____	_____
6.	$420	$8\frac{1}{4}$%	4 years	_____	_____
7.	$750	7%	5 years	_____	_____
8.	$580	$3\frac{1}{4}$%	3 years	_____	_____
9.	$1,300	4%	$3\frac{1}{2}$ years	_____	_____
10.	$1,060	5%	$4\frac{1}{4}$ years	_____	_____
11.	$600	$3\frac{1}{2}$%	$2\frac{3}{4}$ years	_____	_____
12.	$520	$6\frac{1}{2}$%	$5\frac{1}{4}$ years	_____	_____
13.	$880	$4\frac{1}{4}$%	$\frac{3}{4}$ year	_____	_____
14.	$1,500	8%	$\frac{1}{4}$ year	_____	_____
15.	$700	$1\frac{1}{2}$%	$\frac{1}{2}$ year	_____	_____

Check What You Learned

Calculating Interest

Solve each problem.

16. Luis has $660 in his savings account earning $4\frac{1}{2}\%$ interest. How much interest will he earn in 2 years? How much money will be in the account?

Luis will earn _____ in interest.

He will have a total of _____ in his account.

16.

---

17. Mrs. Cole borrowed $1,200 for 6 months ($\frac{1}{2}$ year) at $3\frac{1}{4}\%$ interest. How much interest will she pay? What is the total amount she has to pay?

Mrs. Cole will pay _____ in interest.

She will pay a total of _____.

17.

---

18. Flo invested in a 6-year certificate. If she invested $750 and it pays $5\frac{3}{4}\%$ interest, how much interest will she get? What will the certificate be worth after 6 years?

Flo will get _____ in interest.

The certificate will be worth a total of _____.

18.

---

19. Interest on a $2\frac{1}{2}$ year loan of $920 was charged at the rate of $8\frac{1}{4}\%$ a year. How much interest was charged? What is the total amount to be paid back on the loan?

The interest charged was _____.

A total of _____ must be paid back.

19.

---

20. Juan bought a new computer on credit. He has $\frac{3}{4}$ of a year to repay $890 at 4% interest. How much interest will he pay? What is the total he will be paying for the computer?

Juan will pay _____ in interest.

He will pay a total of _____.

20.

Check What You Know

Ratio and Proportion

Solve each of the following.

	a	b	c

1. $\frac{8}{15} = \frac{24}{n}$ _____ $\frac{3}{6} = \frac{n}{2}$ _____ $\frac{7}{n} = \frac{14}{16}$ _____

2. $\frac{8}{n} = \frac{1}{3}$ _____ $\frac{n}{10} = \frac{4}{8}$ _____ $\frac{6}{n} = \frac{16}{24}$ _____

3. $\frac{n}{25} = \frac{2}{5}$ _____ $\frac{4}{25} = \frac{n}{100}$ _____ $\frac{32}{16} = \frac{2}{n}$ _____

4. $\frac{9}{5} = \frac{n}{20}$ _____ $\frac{18}{54} = \frac{1}{n}$ _____ $\frac{50}{75} = \frac{n}{6}$ _____

5. $\frac{n}{3} = \frac{16}{6}$ _____ $\frac{20}{60} = \frac{n}{33}$ _____ $\frac{42}{n} = \frac{12}{2}$ _____

Check What You Know

SHOW YOUR WORK

Ratio and Proportion

Solve each problem.

6. Three baskets of oranges weigh 120 pounds. How many pounds are in 4 baskets?

   There are _____ pounds in 4 baskets.

   6.

7. A scale drawing of a car is 3 inches to 12 inches. If the car is 48 inches high, how high is the drawing?

   The drawing is _____ inches high.

   7.

8. There are 60 pencils in 4 pencil boxes. How many pencils are in 7 boxes?

   There are _____ pencils in 7 boxes.

   8.

9. The supply store sells 4 pencils for every 5 pens. The store sold 28 pencils yesterday. How many pens did it sell?

   The store sold _____ pens.

   9.

10. The ratio of chaperones to students on a field trip is 2 to 9. If 252 students went on the trip, how many chaperones were there?

    There were _____ chaperones on the field trip.

    10.

11. On a map, each inch represents 25 miles. What is the length of a highway if it is 6 inches long on a map?

    The highway is _____ miles long.

    11.

12. A survey found that 3 out of 8 students have pets. If 27 students have pets, how many students were surveyed?

    _____ students were surveyed.

    12.

Lesson 6.1 Ratio and Proportion

A **ratio** is a comparison of two numbers. A **proportion** expresses the equality of two ratios.

A ratio can be expressed as 1 to 2, 1:2, or $\frac{1}{2}$, and it means that for every 1 of the first item, there are 2 of the other item.

Cross-multiply to determine if two ratios are equal.

$$\frac{2}{4}, \frac{3}{6} \qquad 2 \times 6 = 12 \qquad 3 \times 4 = 12 \qquad \frac{2}{4} = \frac{3}{6}$$

Circle the ratios that are equal. Show your work.

	a	b	c
1.	$\frac{1}{3}, \frac{2}{6}$	$\frac{3}{8}, \frac{1}{4}$	$\frac{3}{5}, \frac{9}{15}$
2.	$\frac{3}{4}, \frac{9}{12}$	$\frac{1}{2}, \frac{4}{8}$	$\frac{5}{6}, \frac{15}{18}$
3.	$\frac{5}{8}, \frac{4}{7}$	$\frac{1}{2}, \frac{1}{4}$	$\frac{4}{3}, \frac{16}{12}$
4.	$\frac{6}{18}, \frac{2}{6}$	$\frac{3}{25}, \frac{6}{50}$	$\frac{1}{8}, \frac{2}{10}$
5.	$\frac{1}{4}, \frac{2}{4}$	$\frac{5}{10}, \frac{3}{6}$	$\frac{4}{24}, \frac{7}{42}$
6.	$\frac{3}{5}, \frac{5}{3}$	$\frac{7}{8}, \frac{21}{24}$	$\frac{8}{23}, \frac{9}{46}$
7.	$\frac{7}{4}, \frac{28}{16}$	$\frac{3}{9}, \frac{1}{3}$	$\frac{16}{20}, \frac{9}{10}$
8.	$\frac{8}{100}, \frac{80}{50}$	$\frac{8}{12}, \frac{10}{14}$	$\frac{15}{20}, \frac{3}{4}$
9.	$\frac{9}{2}, \frac{12}{3}$	$\frac{6}{3}, \frac{8}{4}$	$\frac{1}{3}, \frac{11}{33}$
10.	$\frac{12}{7}, \frac{36}{21}$	$\frac{10}{12}, \frac{15}{20}$	$\frac{3}{4}, \frac{9}{16}$

Lesson 6.2 Solving Proportion Problems

A proportion can be used in problem solving.

The ratio of apples to oranges is 4 to 5. There are 20 oranges in the basket. How many apples are there?

$\frac{4}{5} = \frac{n}{20}$ Set up a proportion, using n for the missing number.

$4 \times 20 = 5 \times n$ Cross-multiply.

$\frac{80}{5} = n$ Solve for n.

$16 = n$ There are 16 apples.

Solve each of the following.

	a	b	c
1.	$\frac{1}{3} = \frac{n}{24}$ _____	$\frac{4}{9} = \frac{n}{36}$ _____	$\frac{5}{45} = \frac{n}{9}$ _____
2.	$\frac{3}{5} = \frac{n}{15}$ _____	$\frac{10}{70} = \frac{n}{7}$ _____	$\frac{25}{40} = \frac{n}{16}$ _____
3.	$\frac{7}{12} = \frac{n}{36}$ _____	$\frac{13}{26} = \frac{n}{4}$ _____	$\frac{7}{1} = \frac{n}{3}$ _____
4.	$\frac{8}{5} = \frac{n}{40}$ _____	$\frac{2}{6} = \frac{n}{33}$ _____	$\frac{5}{13} = \frac{n}{39}$ _____
5.	$\frac{5}{6} = \frac{n}{18}$ _____	$\frac{9}{8} = \frac{n}{32}$ _____	$\frac{2}{3} = \frac{n}{15}$ _____

Lesson 6.3 | Solving Proportion Problems

The missing number can appear any place in a proportion.
Solve the same way.

$\frac{2}{3} = \frac{6}{n}$

$3 \times 6 = 2 \times n$

$\frac{18}{2} = n$

$9 = n$

$\frac{3}{5} = \frac{n}{10}$

$3 \times 10 = 5 \times n$

$\frac{30}{5} = n$

$6 = n$

$\frac{3}{n} = \frac{6}{8}$

$3 \times 8 = 6 \times n$

$\frac{24}{6} = n$

$4 = n$

$\frac{n}{4} = \frac{3}{6}$

$4 \times 3 = 6 \times n$

$\frac{12}{6} = n$

$2 = n$

Solve each of the following.

	a	b	c
1.	$\frac{n}{3} = \frac{3}{9}$ _____	$\frac{5}{3} = \frac{15}{n}$ _____	$\frac{2}{n} = \frac{1}{4}$ _____
2.	$\frac{15}{30} = \frac{2}{n}$ _____	$\frac{4}{6} = \frac{n}{24}$ _____	$\frac{n}{7} = \frac{15}{21}$ _____
3.	$\frac{6}{n} = \frac{15}{20}$ _____	$\frac{n}{12} = \frac{9}{18}$ _____	$\frac{9}{2} = \frac{27}{n}$ _____
4.	$\frac{7}{9} = \frac{n}{63}$ _____	$\frac{15}{n} = \frac{12}{4}$ _____	$\frac{40}{100} = \frac{n}{25}$ _____
5.	$\frac{35}{n} = \frac{4}{8}$ _____	$\frac{16}{4} = \frac{36}{n}$ _____	$\frac{n}{12} = \frac{25}{30}$ _____

Lesson 6.4   Problem Solving

SHOW YOUR WORK

Solve each problem.

1. The ratio of cars to minivans in the parking lot is 2 to 3. There are 96 minivans. How many cars are in the lot?

There are _____ cars in the lot.

1.

2. The ratio of skateboards to bicycles at the park is 5 to 2. If there are 12 bicycles, how many skateboards are there?

There are _____ skateboards.

2.

3. An ice cream shop sells 4 vanilla cones for every 3 chocolate cones. The store sold 48 vanilla cones today. How many chocolate cones did it sell?

The store sold _____ chocolate cones.

3.

4. A flower arrangement has 8 carnations for every 4 roses. There are 14 carnations. How many roses are in the arrangement?

There are _____ roses in the arrangement.

4.

5. There are 18 girls in the school choir. The ratio of girls to boys is 1 to 2. How many boys are in the choir?

There are _____ boys in the choir.

5.

6. A baseball player strikes out 3 times for every 2 hits he gets. If the player strikes out 15 times, how many hits does he get? If the player gets 46 hits, how many times does he strike out?

The player gets _____ hits for every 15 times he strikes out.

If the player gets 46 hits, he strikes out _____ times.

6.

Lesson 6.5 Proportions and Scale Drawings

A **scale drawing** is a drawing of a real object in which all of the dimensions are proportional to the real object. A scale drawing can be larger or smaller than the object it represents. The **scale** is the ratio of the drawing size to the actual size of the object.

A drawing of a person has a scale of 2 inches = 1 foot. If the drawing is 11 inches high, how tall is the person?

$$L\frac{2}{1} = L\frac{11}{n}$$ Write a proportion.

$$\frac{1 \times 11}{2} = n$$ Solve for n.

$$5\frac{1}{2} = n$$ The person is $5\frac{1}{2}$ feet tall.

SHOW YOUR WORK

Solve each problem. Write a proportion in the space to the right.

1. A bridge is 440 yards long. A scale drawing has a ratio of 1 inch = 1 yard. How long is the drawing?

   The drawing is _____ inches long.

   1.

2. A map of the county uses a scale of 2 inches = 19 miles. If the county is 76 miles wide, how wide is the map?

   The map is _____ inches wide.

   2.

3. A picture of a goldfish has a scale of 8 centimeters to 3 centimeters. If the actual goldfish is 12 centimeters long, how long is the drawing?

   The drawing is _____ centimeters long.

   3.

4. An architect made a scale drawing of a house to be built. The scale is 2 inches to 3 feet. The house in the drawing is 24 inches tall. How tall is the actual house?

   The actual house is _____ feet tall.

   4.

Lesson 6.6 Problem Solving

Solve each problem.

1. The proportion of nickels to dimes in a coin jar is 2 to 5. If there are 35 dimes, how many nickels are there?

   There are _____ nickels in the jar.

2. On a map, each centimeter represents 45 kilometers. Two towns are 135 kilometers apart. What is the distance between the towns on the map?

   The towns are _____ centimeters apart on the map.

3. A certain recipe calls for 2 cups of flour and 3 ounces of oil. If the recipe is increased to use 8 cups of flour, how much oil should be used?

   _____ ounces of oil should be used.

4. An 8-inch by 12-inch portrait is reduced to be "pocket size." If the shorter side is now 2 inches, how long is the longer side?

   The longer side is _____ inches.

5. Tim practices guitar 3 hours for every 1 hour he plays basketball. He practiced guitar 24 hours last month. How many hours did he play basketball?

   Tim played basketball _____ hours last month.

6. The shipping charge on a 30-pound package is $6. How much would the shipping cost be on a 50-pound package?

   The shipping cost would be _____.

7. A new school has a teacher-to-student ratio of 2:15. The school has 42 teachers. How many students are there in the school?

   There are _____ students in the school.

1.

2.

3.

4.

5.

6.

7.

Check What You Learned

Ratio and Proportion

Solve each of the following.

a	b	c

1. $\frac{3}{2} = \frac{n}{6}$ _____ $\frac{17}{34} = \frac{1}{n}$ _____ $\frac{n}{16} = \frac{6}{4}$ _____

2. $\frac{7}{n} = \frac{21}{12}$ _____ $\frac{5}{8} = \frac{n}{40}$ _____ $\frac{1}{2} = \frac{56}{n}$ _____

3. $\frac{n}{12} = \frac{2}{3}$ _____ $\frac{9}{n} = \frac{12}{8}$ _____ $\frac{36}{50} = \frac{n}{100}$ _____

4. $\frac{24}{3} = \frac{8}{n}$ _____ $\frac{n}{9} = \frac{4}{12}$ _____ $\frac{6}{n} = \frac{18}{75}$ _____

5. $\frac{5}{2} = \frac{n}{12}$ _____ $\frac{4}{2} = \frac{32}{n}$ _____ $\frac{3}{n} = \frac{15}{20}$ _____

Check What You Learned

Ratio and Proportion

Solve each problem.

6. Three out of every 7 houses in the neighborhood are painted white. There are 224 houses in the neighborhood. How many houses are white?

There are _____ white houses in the neighborhood.

6.

7. A plan for a new development is created as a scale drawing. On the plan, 8 centimeters equal 75 meters. The width of the development is 675 meters. How wide is the plan drawing?

The drawing is _____ centimeters wide.

7.

8. A 6-inch by 4-inch photograph is enlarged so that the shorter side is 26 inches. How long is the longer side?

The longer side is _____ inches.

8.

9. There are 9 chairs for every 2 tables in the lunchroom. There are 81 chairs. How many tables are there?

There are _____ tables in the lunchroom.

9.

10. Lois spends 3 hours doing French homework for every 2 hours she spends on history. Last month, she had 24 hours of history homework. How many hours of French homework did she have?

She had _____ hours of French homework.

10.

11. Six buckets of gravel weigh 48 pounds. How much would 4 buckets weigh?

Four buckets of gravel would weigh _____ pounds.

11.

12. On a map, a road is 7 inches long. If the scale is 1 inch = 14 miles, how long is the actual road?

The actual road is _____ miles long.

12.

Mid-Test Chapters 1–6

Add, subtract, multiply, or divide. Write each answer in simplest form.

	a	b	c	d
1.	$\begin{array}{r} 127 \\ 46 \\ +352 \\ \hline \end{array}$	$\begin{array}{r} 2079 \\ 114 \\ +\ \ 17 \\ \hline \end{array}$	$\begin{array}{r} 5\frac{1}{2} \\ +7\frac{2}{3} \\ \hline \end{array}$	$\begin{array}{r} 3\frac{7}{8} \\ +2\frac{2}{5} \\ \hline \end{array}$
2.	$\begin{array}{r} 346 \\ -\ \ 72 \\ \hline \end{array}$	$\begin{array}{r} 480 \\ -119 \\ \hline \end{array}$	$\begin{array}{r} 6\frac{2}{9} \\ -3\frac{1}{4} \\ \hline \end{array}$	$\begin{array}{r} 5\frac{1}{2} \\ -2\frac{3}{7} \\ \hline \end{array}$
3.	$\begin{array}{r} 275 \\ \times\ \ 56 \\ \hline \end{array}$	$\begin{array}{r} 312 \\ \times\ \ \ 9 \\ \hline \end{array}$	$\begin{array}{r} 1717 \\ \times\ \ \ \ 34 \\ \hline \end{array}$	$\begin{array}{r} 5806 \\ \times\ \ \ \ 42 \\ \hline \end{array}$
4.	$\frac{1}{4} \times \frac{5}{6}$	$\frac{3}{8} \times \frac{2}{3}$	$2\frac{5}{7} \times \frac{4}{9}$	$\frac{1}{2} \times \frac{3}{5} \times \frac{2}{3}$
5.	$8\overline{)72}$	$19\overline{)384}$	$52\overline{)6147}$	$8\overline{)1352}$
6.	$\frac{2}{3} \div \frac{4}{7}$	$3\frac{1}{2} \div \frac{5}{6}$	$\frac{4}{9} \div \frac{1}{12}$	$2\frac{2}{3} \div 1\frac{1}{8}$

Mid-Test Chapters 1–6

Add, subtract, multiply, or divide.

	a	b	c	d

7.

a	b	c	d
1 4	7 2 0 2 4	5.7 3	2 8.3 0 5 2
5 1 3 8	3 1 5 6 4 2	0.2 1 2	1.0 7 1
+ 2 0 3	+ 1 3 5 7	+ 1.6	+ 5.5 8

8.

a	b	c	d
5 8 6 4 2 3	4 3 2 4 8	4 2.5	7.2 8
− 7 9 8 2	− 1 9 1 5 6	− 1 6.3 0 4	− 0.9 5 9

9.

a	b	c	d
5 8 6	2.1	3.5 0 7	3 8.2
× 3.7	× 0.8	× 2.6	× 7.5 8

10.

a	b	c	d
9 8	3 7 0	7.0 2 1 5	4 2.3 6
× 0.4	× 6.4	× 9	× 1 3

11. 2.5)‾10‾   0.03)‾36‾   9)‾7.2‾   8)‾5.664‾

12. 4.8)‾24.96‾   0.37)‾2.2755‾   9.06)‾66.138‾   1.205)‾4.2175‾

Mid-Test Chapters 1–6

Change to percents.

	a	**b**	**c**
13.	$\frac{3}{20} =$ _____ %	$\frac{4}{5} =$ _____ %	$\frac{14}{50} =$ _____ %

Change to decimals.

14. $30\% =$ _____ $72\frac{1}{4}\% =$ _____ $346\% =$ _____

Change to fractions.

15. $75\% =$ _____ $20\% =$ _____ $140\% =$ _____

Complete.

16. _____ is 9% of 30.   _____ is 8% of 15.   _____ is 22% of 90.

17. 36.9 is 45% of _____.   0.36 is 12% of _____.   120 is 150% of _____.

18. 13 is _____% of 52.   5 is _____% of 125.   38 is _____% of 40.

Complete the following.

	Principal	**Rate**	**Time**	**Interest**	**Total Amount**
19.	$720	$3\frac{1}{4}\%$	4 years	_____	_____
20.	$500	$5\frac{1}{2}\%$	$3\frac{1}{2}$ years	_____	_____
21.	$60	4%	$\frac{3}{4}$ year	_____	_____
22.	$480	$12\frac{1}{2}\%$	$5\frac{1}{4}$ years	_____	_____

Mid-Test Chapters 1–6

Solve each problem.

23. A can of mixed nuts has 5 peanuts for every 2 cashews. There are 175 peanuts in the can. How many cashews are there?

There are _____ cashews in the can.

24. A savings account pays $4\frac{1}{2}\%$ interest. How much interest will be earned on $450 in 3 years? How much money will be in the account in 3 years?

The account will earn _____ in interest in 3 years.

There will be _____ in the account in 3 years.

25. A drawing of an office building has a scale of 2 inches = 30 feet. The building is 105 feet tall. How tall is the drawing?

The drawing is _____ inches tall.

26. A company charges $2\frac{1}{4}\%$ for shipping and handling on all purchases. How much is shipping and handling on a purchase of $180? What is the total cost to the customer?

The shipping and handling charge is _____.

The total cost to the customer is _____.

27. The Kendalls make monthly deposits into their savings plan. In 7 months, they have deposited $224. If they continue at this rate, how much will they have deposited in 12 months?

They will have deposited _____.

28. During the first half of his shift, a server made $63 in tips on bills totaling $350. At this rate, what will be his total tips if the bills for the evening total $775? What percent was the server tipped?

His total tips will be _____.

The server was tipped _____%.

23.

24.

25.

26.

27.

28.

Check What You Know

Customary Measurement

Convert the following.

	a	b	c
1.	14 yd. = _____ ft.	$4\frac{1}{4}$ mi. = _____ yd.	$2\frac{1}{2}$ mi. = _____ ft.
2.	2.5 ft. = _____ in.	81 ft. = _____ yd.	5940 ft. = _____ mi.
3.	16 yd. 2 ft. = _____ ft.	7 ft. 3 in. = _____ in.	1 mi., 320 ft. = _____ ft.
4.	8052 yd. = _____ mi.	69 in. = ____ ft. ____ in.	42 yd. = _____ in.

	a	b	c
5.	22 c. = _____ qt.	6.5 pt. = _____ c.	82 c. = _____ gal.
6.	9 qt. = _____ gal.	$13\frac{1}{4}$ gal. = _____ qt.	27 pt. = ____ qt. ____ pt.
7.	43 pt. = _____ c.	6 qt. = _____ pt.	$2\frac{3}{4}$ gal. = _____ pt.
8.	19 c. = ____ pt. ____ c.	13 qt. = ____ gal. ____ qt.	5 gal. 2 qt. = _____ qt.

	a	b	c
9.	24 oz. = _____ lb.	2400 lb. = _____ T.	5.5 lb. = _____ oz.
10.	6.25 T. = _____ lb.	13 lb. = _____ oz.	1500 lb. = _____ T.
11.	6200 lb. = _____ T.	12 oz. = _____ lb.	2.6 T. = _____ lb.
12.	18 oz. = ____ lb. ____ oz.	40 oz. = ____ lb. ____ oz.	0.25 lb. = _____ oz.

	a	b	c
13.	$5\frac{1}{2}$ hr. = _____ min.	380 sec. = _____ min.	0.25 hr. = _____ sec.
14.	108 hr. = _____ days	72 min. = _____ hr.	204 hr. = ____ days ____ hr.
15.	560 sec. = ____ min. ____ sec.	3.25 days = _____ hr.	23 min. = _____ sec.
16.	2.5 days = _____ min.	18 hr. = _____ days	15 hr. = _____ min.

Check What You Know

SHOW YOUR WORK

Customary Measurement

Solve each problem.

17. Betsy kept track of her homework minutes by subject for one month. Her results were: English: 443 minutes; history: 474 minutes; math: 382 minutes; science: 527 minutes; Spanish: 438 minutes. How long did she study each subject, in hours and minutes? How many total days, hours, and minutes did she study?

17.

English: _____ hours _____ minutes

History: _____ hours _____ minutes

Math: _____ hours _____ minutes

Science: _____ hours _____ minutes

Spanish: _____ hours _____ minutes

Total: _____ day _____ hours _____ minutes

18. The Linders invited 38 people to a cookout. They need 6 ounces of meat per person. How many total ounces do they need? How many pounds is that?

18.

The Linders need _____ ounces. That is _____ pounds.

19. The Linders in **problem 18** also want to have 3 cups of lemonade for each person. How many quarts do they need? How many gallons is that?

19.

The Linders need _____ quarts. That is _____ gallons.

20. The Linders in **problem 18** want to use 10.5 feet of their patio for the food serving area. Express that in yards, feet, and inches.

20.

The serving area will be _____ yards _____ foot

_____ inches.

21. The walking path at the park is 1,254 feet. If Paul walks the path 8 times, how many miles will he walk?

21.

Paul will walk _____ miles.

Lesson 7.1   Units of Length (inches, feet, yards, and mile)

1 foot (ft.) = 12 inches (in.)	Use the table and multiply or divide to convert units of measure.
1 yard (yd.) = 3 ft. = 36 in.	
1 mile (mi.) = 1760 yd. = 5280 ft.	
3.2 ft. = _____ in.	4224 yd. = _____ mi.
3.2 ft. = (3.2 × 12) = 38.4 in.	4224 yd. ÷ 1760 = 2.4 mi.

Convert the following.

	a	b	c
1.	17 yd. = _____ ft.	8 mi. = _____ ft.	5280 yd. = _____ mi.
2.	280.8 in. = _____ yd.	8.5 mi. = _____ yd.	708 in. = _____ ft.
3.	3 yd. 1 ft. = _____ in.	111 ft. = _____ yd.	12 mi. = _____ yd.
4.	4 mi. 182 yd. = _____ yd.	13 ft. 5 in. = _____ in.	2.4 mi. = _____ ft.
5.	328 in. = ___ yd. ___ in.	41.6 mi. = _____ yd.	22000 yd. = _____ mi.
6.	64.4 ft. = _____ in.	37.8 mi. = _____ ft.	2 mi. 311 ft. = _____ ft.

SHOW YOUR WORK

Solve each problem.

7. The race track at the high school is 0.25 miles long. How many yards is it?

The track is _____ yards long.

7.

8. Lisa swam in the 600-foot race at the swim meet. How many yards is this race?

The race is _____ yards.

8.

9. Rich measured 1.6 miles from his house to the library. How many yards is this? How many feet?

The distance is _____ yards or _____ feet.

9.

Lesson 7.2   Liquid Volume (cups, pints, quarts, gallons)

1 pint (pt.) = 2 cups (c.)

1 quart (qt.) = 2 pt. = 4 c.

1 gallon (gal.) = 4 qt. = 8 pt. = 16 c.

Use the table and multiply or divide to convert units of measure.

11 pt. = _____ c.

11 pt. = (11 × 2) c.

11 pt. = 22 c.

12 pt. = _____ gal.

12 pt. = (12 ÷ 8) gal.

12 pt. = 1.5 gal.

Convert the following.

	a	**b**	**c**
1.	13 c. = _____ pt.	2.5 gal. = _____ qt.	7 qt. = _____ pt.
2.	72 c. = _____ gal.	4 qt. 1 pt. = _____ pt.	5.4 gal. = _____ qt.
3.	3 gal. = _____ pt.	8.5 qt. = _____ c.	11 qt. = ____ gal. ____ qt.
4.	32 c. = _____ qt.	5.25 gal. = _____ c.	27 c. = ____ pt. ____ c.
5.	9.5 pt. = _____ qt.	9.5 qt. = _____ pt.	33 pt. = ____ gal. ____ pt.

SHOW YOUR WORK

Solve each problem.

6. A serving size is 1 cup of orange juice. How many servings are in a $\frac{1}{2}$ gallon bottle?

   There are _____ servings in the bottle.

6.

7. If a teakettle holds 1.75 quarts of water, how many cups of tea can be made?

   _____ cups of tea can be made.

7.

8. Rey's bathtub holds 42 gallons of water. How many quarts is this? How many pints?

   The bathtub holds ____ quarts. It holds ____ pints.

8.

Lesson 7.3 Problem Solving

Solve each problem.

1. The instructions on a package of garden fertilizer say to mix a spoonful of the powder with 9 pints of water. How many cups would this make? How many quarts? How many gallons?

This would make _____ cups.

This would make _____ quarts.

This would make _____ gallons.

1.

2. In an 880 relay race, 4 runners on a team each run 880 yards. How many total yards is this race? How many feet is this? How many miles is this?

This is _____ yards.

This is _____ feet.

This is _____ miles.

2.

3. Bill is 58 inches tall. Nikki is 4.75 feet tall. Elias is 1.5 yards tall. How tall are Bill, Nikki, and Elias in feet and inches? Who is the tallest?

Bill is _____ feet _____ inches.

Nikki is _____ feet _____ inches.

Elias is _____ feet _____ inches.

_____ is the tallest.

3.

4. June needs to buy gas for her lawn mower. Her gas can holds 5.75 quarts. How many gallons is that?

The gas can holds _____ gallons.

4.

5. A water pitcher holds 0.75 gallons of water. How many pints is this? How many cups?

The pitcher holds _____ pints.

The pitcher holds _____ cups.

5.

Lesson 7.4   Weight (ounces, pounds, tons)

1 pound (lb.) = 16 ounces (oz.)	Multiply or divide to convert units of measure.
1 ton (T.) = 2000 lb. = 32000 oz.	

3.6 lb. = _____ oz.   11000 lb. = _____ T.

3.6 lb. = (3.6 × 16) oz.   11000 lb. = (11000 ÷ 2000) lb.

3.6 lb. = 57.6 oz.   11000 lb. = 5.5 T.

Convert the following.

	a	b	c
1.	3.5 T. = _____ lb.	72 oz. = _____ lb.	$\frac{3}{4}$ lb. = _____ oz.
2.	9000 lb. = _____ T.	64000 oz. = _____ T.	430 oz. = _____ lb.
3.	10689 lb. = ___ T. ___ lb.	$3\frac{1}{4}$ lb. = _____ oz.	3800 lb. = _____ T.
4.	9 lb. 14 oz. = _____ oz.	24700 lb. = _____ T.	6.8 T. = _____ lb.
5.	519 oz. = ___ lb. ___ oz.	6.5 lb. = _____ oz.	13 T. = _____ lb.

SHOW YOUR WORK

Solve each problem.

6. A dump truck can carry 3,200 pounds of dirt. How many tons is that?

   The truck can carry _____ tons.

6.

7. At his last veterinary visit, Jerry's cat weighed 12.8 pounds. How many ounces is that?

   Jerry's cat weighed _____ ounces.

7.

8. For the class picnic, the class needs one 4-ounce beef patty for each student. There are 27 students in the class. How many total ounces are needed? How many pounds is that?

   A total of ___ ounces or ___ pounds are needed.

8.

Spectrum Math
Grade 7
88

Chapter 7, Lesson 4
Customary Measurement

Lesson 7.5   Time

1 minute (min.) = 60 seconds (sec.)	Multiply or divide to convert
1 hour (hr.) = 60 min. = 3600 sec.	units of measure.
1 day = 24 hr. = 1440 min.	

75 min. = _____ hr.

75 min. = (75 ÷ 60) hr.

75 min. = 1.25 hr.

16 min. = _____ sec.

16 min. = (16 × 60) sec.

16 min. = 960 sec.

Convert the following.

	a	b	c
1.	12 min. = _____ hr.	900 sec. = _____ min.	3.5 hr. = _____ min.
2.	8 days = _____ hr.	7 min. = _____ sec.	84 hr. = _____ days
3.	320 min. = ___ hr. ___ min.	$5\frac{1}{4}$ hr. = _____ min.	396 sec. = _____ min.
4.	150 hr. = ___ days ___ hr.	1800 sec. = _____ hr.	6.5 hr. = _____ min.
5.	42 days = _____ hr.	3 hr. 15 min. = _____ min.	3.75 min. = _____ sec.

SHOW YOUR WORK

Solve each problem.

6. Jenna swam two laps in 96 seconds. How many minutes did it take her?

It took Jenna _____ minutes to swim two laps.

6.

7. According to the recipe, an apple spice cake has to bake for 90 minutes. How many hours is that?

The cake has to bake _____ hours.

7.

8. Mickey is counting the hours until his trip to the ocean. It is now 228 hours away. How many days and hours are there until the trip?

The trip is in _____ days and _____ hours.

8.

Lesson 7.6 Problem Solving

Solve each problem.

1. Daniel, Trent, and Will competed in a race. Daniel's time was 0.09 hours, Trent's time was 5.8 minutes, and Will's time was 322 seconds. Express each runner's time in minutes and seconds. Who had the fastest time?

   Daniel's time was _____ minutes _____ seconds.

   Trent's time was _____ minutes _____ seconds.

   Will's time was _____ minutes _____ seconds.

   _____ had the fastest time.

2. Bobbie bought 5 bags of trail mix. Each bag weighs 36 ounces. How many pounds of trail mix did she buy?

   Bobbie bought _____ pounds of trail mix.

3. Helen has a washtub that holds 16.5 quarts of water. How many gallons does it hold? How many pints? How many cups?

   The washtub holds _____ gallons.

   It holds _____ pints.

   It holds _____ cups.

4. An engineer determined that it would take $14\frac{1}{2}$ tons of steel to build the structure she designed. How many pounds of steel is that?

   That is _____ pounds of steel.

5. Allen kept track of his time working on his science project. When he added it all up, he found that he spent 138 hours on his science project. How many days is that?

   Allen spent _____ days on his science project.

6. A stationery store sells paper by the pound. Patty bought 4.2 pounds of paper. How many ounces is that?

   Patty bought _____ ounces of paper.

1.

2.

3.

4.

5.

6.

Check What You Learned

Customary Measurement

Convert the following.

	a	b	c
1.	72 ft. = _____ yd.	18 in. = _____ ft.	1.2 mi. = _____ yd.
2.	12.5 yd. = _____ ft.	6600 yd. = _____ mi.	62 ft. = ____ yd. ____ ft.
3.	2 yd. 8 in. = _____ in.	38 yd. = _____ ft.	11880 ft. = _____ mi.
4.	3 mi. 540 yd. = _____ yd.	32.5 ft. = _____ in.	83 ft. = ____ yd. ____ ft.
5.	17 pt. = _____ qt.	6 c. = _____ pt.	41 qt. = _____ gal.
6.	$3\frac{1}{2}$ qt. = _____ c.	2.75 gal. = _____ qt.	3 gal. 5 c. = _____ c.
7.	13 c. = ____ pt. ____ c.	7 qt. = _____ gal.	32 pt. = _____ gal.
8.	8.5 pt. = _____ qt.	3.25 gal. = _____ pt.	4 gal. 3 qt. = _____ qt.
9.	28 oz. = _____ lb.	3.5 T. = _____ lb.	2.5 lb. = _____ oz.
10.	8200 lb. = _____ T.	11 lb. 3 oz. = _____ oz.	54 oz. = _____ lb.
11.	56 oz. = ____ lb. ____ oz.	7.25 T. = _____ lb.	32 oz. = _____ lb.
12.	4.6 lb. = _____ oz.	2.75 T. = _____ lb.	5.25 lb. = _____ oz.
13.	3.5 days = _____ hr.	4 hr. 23 min. = _____ min.	6.25 min. = _____ sec.
14.	210 sec. = _____ min.	88 hr. = ____ days ____ hr.	315 min. = _____ hr.
15.	45 min. = _____ hr.	3.2 min. = _____ sec.	12 hr. = _____ days
16.	6 min. 42 sec. = _____ sec.	8.75 days = __ days __ hr.	6.5 hr. = _____ min.

Check What You Learned

Customary Measurement

Solve each problem.

17. A construction crew removed 6,820 pounds of fill dirt. How much is that in tons and pounds?

The crew removed _____ tons _____ pounds of dirt.

17.

18. It is exactly 1.5 miles from the post office to the bank. How many yards is that? How many feet?

The distance is _____ yards.

The distance is _____ feet.

18.

19. The Jeffersons bought a 45-gallon hot water heater. How many quarts is that? How many cups?

The water heater holds _____ quarts.

It holds _____ cups.

19.

20. There are 18 children in the preschool class, and they each get 1 pint of juice a day. How many total cups is that? How many quarts? How many gallons?

That is _____ cups.

It is _____ quarts.

It is _____ gallons.

20.

21. Shari spent 93 minutes working in her flower garden. She spent 42 minutes trimming the hedges. How many total hours and minutes did she spend working in her yard?

Shari worked _____ hours _____ minutes.

21.

22. Sofia used 18.5 yards of ribbon for a craft project. How many inches is that? How many feet and inches?

Sofia used _____ inches.

That is _____ feet _____ inches.

22.

Check What You Know

Metric Measurement

Convert the following.

	a	**b**
1.	4.8 km = _____ m	1.2 m = _____ cm
2.	0.7 m = _____ mm	2475 m = _____ km
3.	3 cm = _____ mm	682 mm = _____ m
4.	804 mm = _____ cm	13.1 km = _____ m
5.	520 cm = _____ m	480 m = _____ km
6.	2.4 g = _____ mg	6800 kg = _____ MT
7.	12 kg = _____ g	460 mg = _____ g
8.	4.86 MT = _____ kg	2.7 kg = _____ g
9.	743 g = _____ kg	0.8 g = _____ mg
10.	375 kg = _____ MT	2162 mg = _____ g
11.	0.71 kL = _____ L	560 mL = _____ L
12.	87 L = _____ kL	8.94 L = _____ mL
13.	1720 L = _____ kL	346 mL = _____ L
14.	2635 mL = _____ L	500 kL = _____ L
15.	0.63 L = _____ mL	500 L = _____ kL

NAME _____

Check What You Know

Metric Measurement

Solve each problem.

16. A small can of juice is 355 milliliters. A bottle of juice is 1.4 liters. Which holds more, 4 cans or 1 bottle?

_____ hold(s) more.

16.

17. A jar of peanut butter weighs 1.13 kilograms. How many grams is that?

The jar weighs _____ grams.

17.

18. Lucita's house is 743 meters from her cousin's house. Lucita walks to her cousin's house and back home 3 times a week. How many kilometers does she walk in a week?

Lucita walks _____ kilometers.

18.

19. A pen is 147 millimeters long. How many centimeters is that?

The pen is _____ centimeters long.

19.

20. The tanks at a processing plant each hold 651 liters of fluid. There are 7 tanks. In total, how many kiloliters do they hold?

The tanks hold _____ kiloliters.

20.

21. A can of soda contains 40 milligrams of sodium. How many cans would it take to consume a gram of sodium?

It would take _____ cans.

21.

22. A book weighs 723 grams. How much does it weigh in kilograms? in milligrams?

The book weighs _____ kilograms or _____ milligrams.

22.

Lesson 8.1 Units of Length (millimeters, centimeters, meters, and kilometers)

1 centimeter (cm) = 10 millimeters (mm)	1 mm = 0.1 cm = 0.001 m
1 meter (m) = 100 cm = 1000 mm	1 cm = 0.01 m
1 kilometer (km) = 1000 m	1 m = 0.001 km

Multiply to convert units of measure.

23.8 m = _____ cm	23.8 m = _____ mm	23.8 m = _____ km
23.8 m = (23.8 × 100) cm	23.8 m = (23.8 × 1000) mm	23.8 m = (23.8 × 0.001) km
23.8 m = 2380 cm	23.8 m = 23800 mm	23.8 m = 0.0238 km

Convert the following.

	a	b	c
1.	3.5 km = _____ m	4 m = _____ cm	1.1 m = _____ mm
2.	2500 m = _____ km	5200 mm = _____ m	13 cm = _____ mm
3.	0.04 km = _____ m	500 m = _____ mm	230 cm = _____ m
4.	3.27 m = _____ cm	1.6 m = _____ km	18 m = _____ cm
5.	720 cm = _____ m	860 mm = _____ cm	0.75 km = _____ m

SHOW YOUR WORK

Solve each problem.

6. A pencil is 13.6 centimeters long. How many millimeters is that?

   The pencil is _____ millimeters.

6.

7. The bike path is 2,830 meters long. Cindy rode it 4 times. How many kilometers did she ride?

   Cindy rode _____ kilometers.

7.

Lesson 8.2 Liquid Volume (milliliters, liters, and kiloliters)

1 liter (L) = 1000 milliliters (mL)	1 mL = 0.001 liter
1 kiloliter (kL) = 1000 liters	1 liter = 0.001 kL

Multiply to convert units of measure.

8 kL = _____ liters	750 mL = _____ liters
8 kL = (8 × 1000) liters	750 mL = (750 × 0.001) liters
8 kL = 8000 liters	750 mL = 0.75 liters

Convert the following.

	a	b
1.	2.5 kL = _____ L	17 L = _____ mL
2.	560 L = _____ kL	0.82 L = _____ mL
3.	427 mL = _____ L	1.34 kL = _____ L
4.	1826 L = _____ kL	38 mL = _____ L
5.	7.48 L = _____ mL	75 L = _____ kL

SHOW YOUR WORK

Solve each problem.

6. Nick has a scoop that holds 20 milliliters of water. How many scoops will it take to fill a 1 liter container?

It will take _____ scoops.

6.

7. A supplier had 4.3 kiloliters of milk. Customers bought a total of 620 liters this morning. How many kiloliters of milk are left?

There are _____ kiloliters of milk left.

7.

Lesson 8.3 Weight (milligrams, grams, kilograms, and metric tons)

1 gram (g) = 1000 milligrams (mg)	1 mg = 0.001 g
1 kilogram (kg) = 1000 g	1 g = 0.001 kg
1 metric ton (MT) = 1000 kg	1 kg = 0.001 MT

Multiply to convert units of measure.

3.5 kg = _____ g	180 mg = _____ g
3.5 kg = (3.5 × 1000) g	180 mg = (180 × 0.001) g
3.5 kg = 3500 g	180 mg = 0.18 g

Convert the following.

a   b

1. 0.75 kg = _____ g   3410 kg = _____ MT

2. 827 g = _____ kg   8.45 MT = _____ kg

3. 6.2 g = _____ mg   1.3 kg = _____ g

4. 250 kg = _____ MT   630 mg = _____ g

5. 9 kg = _____ g   0.8 g = _____ mg

SHOW YOUR WORK

Solve each problem.

6. One liter of water weighs 1 kilogram. What is the weight in kilograms of 2.75 liters? What is the weight in grams?

The water weighs _____ kilograms or _____ grams.

6.

7. The combined weight of the people on a bus is 1,316 kilograms. How much is that in metric tons?

The people weigh _____ metric tons.

7.

Lesson 8.4 Problem Solving

Solve each problem.

1. Marta is training for the 75-meter dash. She ran the dash 43 times last week. How many meters did she run? How many kilometers?

   Marta ran _____ meters.

   She ran _____ kilometers.

2. Booker is using a 3-liter bucket to fill a 0.81 kiloliter tub. How many buckets will it take to fill the tub?

   It will take _____ buckets.

3. There are 3.6 metric tons of cargo on a cargo ship. How many kilograms is that?

   The ship is carrying _____ kilograms.

4. A table is 193 centimeters long. How many meters is that?

   The table is _____ meters long.

5. A glass holds 450 milliliters of water. A bottle holds 1.5 liters. Which holds more, 3 glasses or 1 bottle?

   _____ hold(s) more.

6. A certain insect weighs about 340 milligrams. How much would a colony of 168 insects weigh, in grams?

   A colony would weigh _____ grams.

7. Pablo is 1.554 meters tall. Ruby is 150 centimeters 48 millimeters tall. Express their height in meters, centimeters, and millimeters. Who is taller?

   Pablo is _____ meter(s), _____ centimeters, and _____ millimeters tall.

   Ruby is _____ meter(s), _____ centimeters, and _____ millimeters tall.

   _____ is taller.

1.
2.
3.
4.
5.
6.
7.

Check What You Learned

Metric Measurement

Convert the following.

a

1. 623 cm = _____ m
2. 211 mm = _____ cm
3. 1.3 cm = _____ mm
4. 0.2 m = _____ mm
5. 3.6 km = _____ m

6. 422 kg = _____ MT
7. 394 g = _____ kg
8. 2.91 MT = _____ kg
9. 8.2 kg = _____ g
10. 9.6 g = _____ mg

11. 0.51 L = _____ mL
12. 6235 mL = _____ L
13. 4807 L = _____ kL
14. 36 L = _____ kL
15. 0.68 kL = _____ L

b

1. 346 m = _____ km
2. 8.7 km = _____ m
3. 512 mm = _____ m
4. 3864 m = _____ km
5. 8.82 m = _____ cm

6. 5847 mg = _____ g
7. 0.24 g = _____ mg
8. 3.12 kg = _____ g
9. 643 mg = _____ g
10. 3425 kg = _____ MT

11. 832 L = _____ kL
12. 26 kL = _____ L
13. 918 mL = _____ L
14. 6.47 liters = _____ mL
15. 390 mL = _____ L

CHAPTER 8 POSTTEST

Check What You Learned

Metric Measurement

Solve each problem.

16. A serving of cereal has 70 milligrams of potassium. The recommended daily allowance of potassium is 3.5 grams. How many servings of cereal would it take to consume that much potassium?

It would take _____ servings of cereal.

16.

17. A small box of clips weighs 215 grams. The giant size box weighs 1.2 kilograms. Which weighs more, 5 small boxes or 1 giant box?

_____ weighs more.

17.

18. The diameter of a nickel is about 2 centimeters. How many nickels would have to be lined up side by side to be 1 meter in length?

It would take _____ nickels to equal 1 meter.

18.

19. A glass holds 420 milliliters and a jar holds 1.47 liters. How many glasses would it take to fill 1 jar?

It would take _____ glasses to fill 1 jar.

19.

20. A spring water company bottled 4,800 bottles of water yesterday. Each bottle holds 0.25 liters. How many kiloliters did they bottle?

The company bottled _____ kiloliters.

20.

21. Alvin's paper route includes 7 streets. Five of the streets are 334 meters long. The other 2 streets are 587 meters long. How many kilometers is Alvin's route?

Alvin's route is _____ kilometers.

21.

22. There were 221 runners in a race. Each runner drank 45 milliliters of water before the race. How many liters did they drink?

The runners drank _____ liters.

22.

Check What You Know

Probability and Statistics

Use the following data set to complete the problems.

Daily High Temperature (°F)

66, 68, 72, 79, 67, 82, 73, 85, 68, 81, 73, 82, 69, 73, 74

1. Make a stem-and-leaf plot for the data.

2. Complete the frequency table to represent the data.

Temperature	Cumulative Frequency	Relative Frequency	Frequency
66°–70°			%
71°–75°			%
76°–80°			%
81°–85°			%

3. Make a line plot to display this data.

4. Make a box-and-whisker plot for this data.

5. Find the mean, median, mode, range, upper extreme, and lower extreme of the data.

        a   **b**

mean: _____   range: _____

median: _____   upper extreme: _____

mode: _____   lower extreme: _____

NAME _____

Check What You Know

Probability and Statistics

6. Pepi's Pizza has a choice of thin crust or thick crust. The available toppings are mushrooms, onions, pepperoni, and sausage. Make a tree diagram showing the possible outcomes for a 1-topping pizza.

Use your tree diagram to answer the following questions.

7. How many possible outcomes are there? _____

8. What is the probability that a pizza will be thin crust? _____

9. What is the probability that a pizza will have onions? _____

10. What is the probability that a pizza will be thick crust and have mushrooms? _____

Use the circle graph at the right to answer the following questions.

11. Which two days combined account for exactly half of the people? _____

12. Which day did the fewest people pick? _____

13. How many people chose Friday? _____

14. What is the angle measure for Saturday? _____

15. Use the data in the circle graph to make a histogram.

What Day Do You Go Grocery Shopping?

20 people responded.

Lesson 9.1 Bar Graphs

Bar graphs are used to compare data that has been collected from two or more data sets. Different colors or patterns are used for the bars to identify each category of a **multiple bar graph**.

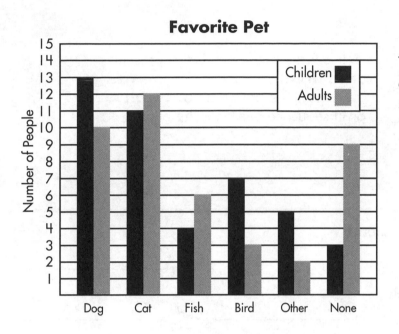

Favorite Pet

This graph shows the favorite pets of adults and children who were surveyed.

Use the bar graph above to answer each question.

1. How many people responded to the survey?   _____

2. How many adults responded? How many children?   adults: _____   children: _____

3. How many adults chose fish?   _____

4. How many children chose cat?   _____

5. How many more adults than children preferred cats?   _____

6. How many more children chose dog than bird?   _____

7. Which pet was chosen by the most adults?   _____

8. Which pet (other than none) was chosen by the fewest children?   _____

9. How many total people chose bird?   _____

Lesson 9.2 Histograms

A **histogram** is a type of bar chart in which the categories are consecutive and the intervals are equal.

Number of Hours Spent Doing Homework Per Week

In this histogram, each bar represents an **interval** of 5 hours. The intervals are equal. The bars are **consecutive**, or in sequence one after the other.

Use the histogram above to answer each question.

1. How many students were surveyed? _____

2. Which two intervals (bars) were selected by an equal number of students? _____ and _____

   How many students chose each of those intervals? _____

3. Which interval was selected by the most students? _____

4. How many more students do 16–20 hours of homework than 1–5 hours? _____

Use the histogram at the right to answer the following questions.

5. Which month had the most snowfall? _____

6. How many inches of snow fell in January through March? _____

7. How many more inches of snow fell in February than in March? _____

8. How many inches of snow fell in December? _____

Snowfall per Month

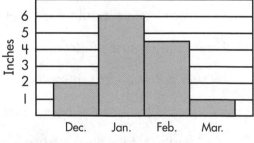

Lesson 9.3   Line Graphs

Line graphs are used to show how a variable changes over time. Multiple lines can be used on the same graph to compare 2 or more variables.

Pitching Record

This graph shows the pitching record for the first 10 baseball games. As shown in the key, a different kind of line is used for each event being recorded.

Use the line graph above to answer the following questions.

1. How many total hits were given up? _____

2. What was the total number of walks? _____

3. Which game had the same number of strikeouts and hits? _____

4. How many games had no walks? _____

5. Which game(s) had 6 strikeouts? _____

6. In which game(s) did the pitcher give up the fewest hits? _____

7. Over the course of 10 games, were there more walks or more strikeouts? _____

8. How many more hits were there in game 5 than in game 4? _____

Lesson 9.4　Circle Graphs

A **circle graph** shows the relationship of parts to a whole. The circle is divided into sectors which add up to 100%. The sectors are determined by the central angles, and the sum of all those angles is 360°.

Favorite Gum Flavor

This circle graph shows the favorite gum flavor of 400 people. The sectors show the percent who prefer each flavor.

Use the circle graph above to answer each question.

1. Which flavor is preferred by the most people?　　_____

2. How many people prefer spearmint?　　_____

3. How many people prefer cinnamon?　　_____

4. Which flavor is preferred by the same number of people who prefer cinnamon?　　_____

5. Which two flavors combined account for exactly half of the people?　　_____

6. How many people prefer bubblegum?　　_____

7. What is the measure of the angle for the peppermint sector of the graph?　　_____

8. What is the measure of the angle for the fruit sector of the graph?　　_____

9. What is the measure of the angle for the bubblegum sector of the graph?　　_____

Lesson 9.5 Scattergrams

A **scattergram** shows the relationship between two sets of data. It is made up of points. The points are plotted by using the values from the two sets of data as coordinates.

Note: Before working Lesson 9.5 activities, you may find it helpful to work Lesson 10.11, *Plotting Ordered Pairs.*

Sno-Cone Sales

This scattergram shows the relationship between the temperature and the number of sno-cones sold. As one value increases, the other appears to increase as well. This indicates a *positive* relationship.

A *negative* relationship would show that more sno-cones are sold as the temperature decreases.

No relationship would show no clear trend in the data.

Use the scattergram above to complete the data table. Include the coordinates for all 14 points.

1.

Sno-Cones	12	12	13	14										
Temperature	60	70	60	65										

Does each scattergram below indicate a positive relationship, a negative relationship, or no relationship?

2.

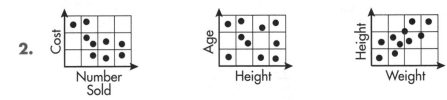

_____   _____   _____

Use the data below to create a scattergram on the grid. Be sure to include all labels.

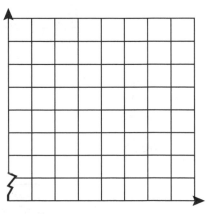

3.

Hours Studying	0.5	0.5	0.75	0.75	1	1	1.25	1.25	1.5	2
Test Grade	71	72	70	76	74	80	82	83	80	85

Lesson 9.6 Measures of Central Tendency

The **mean** is the average of a set of numbers. It is found by adding the set of numbers and then dividing by the number of addends.

The **median** is the middle number of a set of numbers that is ordered from least to greatest. When there is an even amount of numbers, it is the mean of the two middle numbers.

The **mode** is the number that appears most often in a set of numbers. There is no mode if all numbers appear the same number of times.

The **range** is the difference between the greatest and least numbers in the set.

Find the mean, median, mode, and range of the following set of numbers.

34, 32, 39, 33, 37, 36, 39, 38

mean: $34 + 32 + 39 + 33 + 37 + 36 + 39 + 38 = \frac{288}{8} = 36$

Arrange the numbers from least to greatest to find median, mode, and range.

32, 33, 34, 36, 37, 38, 39, 39

median: $\frac{36+37}{2} = 36.5$ mode: 39   range: $39 - 32 = 7$

Find the mean, median, mode, and range of the following sets of numbers.

	a	b
1.	8, 6, 9, 11, 12, 4, 9, 10, 9, 2	40.7, 23.1, 18.5, 43.6, 52.1, 50.9, 44.8, 23.1

    mean: _____   mean: _____

    median: _____   median: _____

    mode: _____   mode: _____

    range: _____   range: _____

2. 152, 136, 171, 208, 193, 163, 124, 212, 216, 171   349, 562.5, 612, 349, 187, 612, 530, 716.5, 349, 902

    mean: _____   mean: _____

    median: _____   median: _____

    mode: _____   mode: _____

    range: _____   range: _____

Lesson 9.7   Stem-and-Leaf Plots

A **stem-and-leaf** plot is used to arrange data in order from least to greatest. It is displayed in two columns. The right column shows the **leaves**—the ones digit of each number. The other digits form the **stems** and are shown in the left column. The **key** explains how to read the plot.

Use the following data to create a stem-and-leaf plot.

71, 73, 87, 106, 95, 73, 86,

99, 104, 82, 93, 74, 101, 90

Stem	Leaves
7	1 3 3 4
8	2 6 7
9	0 3 5 9
10	1 4 6

Key: 7 | 1 = 71

Create a stem-and-leaf plot for each set of data.

a

b

1. 18, 17, 12, 24, 17, 33, 21, 22, 14, 31, 30, 20, 16, 35

122, 120, 135, 130, 148, 131, 142, 122, 133, 143, 135, 132

2. 32, 46, 21, 33, 51, 65, 22, 45

78, 109, 73, 82, 95, 112, 93, 86, 109

3. 135, 146, 128, 164, 137, 152, 167, 150

346, 327, 368, 342, 339, 351, 346, 329

Lesson 9.8 Frequency Tables

A **frequency table** shows how often an item, a number, or a range of numbers occurs. The **cumulative frequency** is the sum of all frequencies up to and including the current one. The **relative frequency** is the percent of a specific frequency.

Make a frequency table for these test scores:

71, 85, 73, 92, 86, 79, 87,

98, 82, 93, 81, 89, 88, 96

Test Scores

Score	Frequency	Cumulative Frequency	Relative Frequency
71–75	2	2	14.3%
76–80	1	3	7.1%
81–85	3	6	21.4%
86–90	4	10	28.6%
91–95	2	12	14.3%
96–100	2	14	14.3%

Use the following data to complete the frequency table.

1. Cats' weights:

9.4375 lb., 11.375 lb., 12.1875 lb., 11.625 lb., 8.625 lb., 9.6875 lb., 8.875 lb., 12.5 lb., 9.375 lb., 10.25 lb., 10.625 lb., 12.0625 lb., 11.875 lb., 8.9375 lb., 9.75 lb., 10.1875 lb., 10.125 lb., 10.1875 lb., 12.0 lb., 9.125 lb.

Cats' Weights

Weight in pounds	Frequency	Cumulative Frequency	Relative Frequency
8.6–8.99			%
9–9.5			%
9.6–9.99			%
10–10.5			%
10.6–10.99			%
11–11.5			%
11.6–11.99			%
12–12.5			%

Answer the following questions about the frequency table above.

2. How many cats weigh 12–12.5 pounds? _____

3. How many cats weigh 10.6–10.99 pounds? _____

4. How many cats weigh less than 10 pounds? _____

5. How many cats weigh 11 pounds or more? _____

6. What percent of cats is 10–10.5 pounds? _____

7. What percent of cats is less than 9 pounds? _____

Lesson 9.9 Line Plots

A **line plot** is a graph that shows the frequency of data on a number line. Line plots make it easy to identify the mode, range, and any outliers in a data set. **Outliers** are data points that are much larger or smaller than other values.

To make a line plot, draw a number line from the least to the greatest value in the number set. Then, make an x above each number every time it appears in the set.

Make a line plot for the following data:

8, 9, 11, 8, 10, 11, 8, 9, 12, 8, 17, 12

The mode is 8. The range is $17 - 8 = 9$.
17 is an outlier.

```
X
X
X     X         X   X
X  X  X   X  X  X              X
+--+--+--+--+--+--+--+--+--+--+--+--+
 7  8  9 10 11 12 13 14 15 16 17 18
```

Answer the questions about the line plots below.

1. How many people responded to
   the sibling survey?   _____

2. What is the mode of the sibling survey?
   What is the range?

   mode: _____   range: _____

3. How many people have 3 or more siblings?   _____

4. What number is an outlier on the sibling survey?   _____

Number of Siblings

```
      X
      X
      X   X
   X  X   X      X
   X  X   X   X  X   X           X
+--+--+--+--+--+--+--+--+--+--+
 0  1  2  3  4  5  6  7  8  9 10
```

5. How many people responded to the
   test survey?   _____

6. What is the mode of the test survey?
   What is the range?

   mode: _____   range: _____

7. How many people studied 2 or fewer hours?   _____

8. How many people studied 4 or more hours?   _____

9. Did more people study 2 or more hours or less than 2 hours?

   More people studied _____ hours.

Hours Studying For Test

```
                X
                X   X              X
                X   X              X
         X      X   X      X   X   X
   X     X      X   X   X  X   X   X
+--+----+----+----+----+----+----+----+
   ½     1   1½   2   2½   3   3½   4
```

Lesson 9.10 Box-and-Whisker Plots

A **box-and-whisker** plot displays data along a number line. Quartiles are used to divide the data into four equal parts. Each quartile is 25% of the number of items. The upper and lower quartiles, representing 50% of the data, form the box. The upper extreme (highest value) and lower extreme (lowest value) form the whiskers.

This box-and-whisker plot represents the following data:

12, 13, 14, 14, 15, 16, 17, 18, 19, 19, 21

Upper Extreme: 21   Upper Quartile (median of upper half): 19

Lower Extreme: 12   Lower Quartile (median of lower half): 14

Middle Quartile (median): 16

Use the box-and-whisker plots below to answer the following questions.

1. What is the median number of miles walked? _____

   Miles Walked in Walk-a-Thon

2. What are the lowest and highest numbers of miles walked?

   lowest: _____   highest: _____

3. If 126 people participated in the walkathon, how many people walked 7–10 miles? _____

4. What percentage of the people walked more than 10 miles? _____

---

5. What is the median number of books read? _____

   Books Read Over the Summer

6. What is the upper quartile? _____

7. What percentage of the people who responded to the survey read 4 or fewer books? _____

8. What is the most number of books anyone read? _____

9. If 82 people responded to this survey, how many read from 4 to 18 books? _____

Lesson 9.11   Tree Diagrams

A **sample space** is a set of all possible outcomes (or possible results) for an activity or experiment. To determine the sample space, it is helpful to organize the possibilities using a list, chart, picture, or tree diagram.

Show the sample space for tossing a nickel, a dime, and a quarter.

Nickel	Dime	Quarter	Possible Outcomes
		H	HHH
	H	T	HHT
Heads (H)		H	HTH
	T	T	HTT
	H	H	THH
Tails (T)		T	THT
	T	H	TTH
		T	TTT

There are 8 possible outcomes or possible results.

Make a tree diagram for each situation. Determine the number of possible outcomes.

1. The concession stand offers the drink choices shown in the table.

Drinks	Sizes
Lemonade	Small
Fruit Punch	Medium
Apple Cider	Large
	Jumbo

There are _____ possible outcomes.

2. The Kellys are planning their vacation activities. The first day they can go to the zoo or the museum. The second day they can go to the pier or the dunes. The third day they have to choose sailing, swimming, or horseback riding.

There are _____ possible outcomes.

Lesson 9.12   Calculating Probability

An **outcome** is any of the possible results of an activity or experiment. **Probability** is the likelihood that a specific outcome or set of outcomes will occur. Probability is the ratio of desired outcome(s) to the sample space. It can be expressed as a ratio, fraction, decimal, or percent.

When tossing a coin, what is the probability that it will land on heads?

desired outcome: heads   sample space: heads, tails   probability: 1:2, $\frac{1}{2}$, 50%, 0.5

Find the probability. Express your answer as a fraction in simplest form.

A box contains 3 red pencils, 4 blue pencils, 2 green pencils, and 1 regular pencil. If you take 1 pencil without looking, what is the probability of picking each of the following?

1. a red pencil _____

2. a blue pencil _____

3. a green pencil _____

4. a regular pencil _____

If you spin the spinner shown at the right, what is the probability of the spinner stopping on each of the following?

5. a letter _____

6. an odd number _____

7. an even number _____

8. a vowel _____

9. the number 3 _____

10. a consonant _____

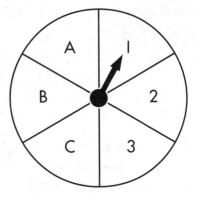

Check What You Learned

Probability and Statistics

Use the following data set to complete the problems.

Number of Cars Across the Bridge

93, 105, 92, 111, 98, 97, 108, 101, 112, 115, 96, 104, 103, 91, 97

1. Make a stem-and-leaf plot to represent the data.

2. Make a frequency table for this data.

3. Make a line plot to display this data.

4. Make a box-and-whisker plot for this data.

5. Find the mean, median, mode, range, upper quartile, and lower quartile for this data.

a	b

mean: _____   range: _____

median: _____   upper quartile: _____

mode: _____   lower quartile: _____

Check What You Learned

Probability and Statistics

6. Paul is getting a new bike. He can get either a racing bike or a mountain bike. His color choices are red, black, and silver. Make a tree diagram showing Paul's possible outcomes.

Use your tree diagram to answer the following questions.

7. How many possible outcomes are there? _____

8. What is the probability that Paul will get a racing bike? _____

9. What is the probability that the bike will be red? _____

10. What is the probability that Paul will get a silver mountain bike? _____

Use the circle graph at the right to answer the following questions.

11. How many people exercise 10–12 hours per week? _____

12. What is the angle measure for 7–9 hours? _____

13. How many hours do the most people exercise? _____

14. Which group can be combined with the people who exercise 7–9 hours to account for exactly half of the people? _____

15. Use the data in the circle graph to make a histogram.

Hours of Exercise Per Week

40 people responded.

Check What You Know

Geometry

Identify the following.

	a	**b**	**c**
1.	•T _____	R ——— S _____	

2. _____   _____   _____

Name the angle, rays, and vertex.

3.

angle: _____   rays: _____   vertex: _____

4.

angle: _____   rays: _____   vertex: _____

Use the figure at the right to complete the following.

5. Which two lines are parallel? _____

6. If ∠4 is 120°, What is the measure of ∠3? _____

7. Is ∠3 acute, obtuse, or right? _____

8. What angle is vertical to ∠11? _____

9. What angle is supplementary to ∠6? _____

Name the transversal that forms each pair of angles. Write whether the angles are alternate interior, alternate exterior, or corresponding.

10. ∠4 and ∠6   _____   _____

11. ∠15 and ∠9   _____   _____

12. ∠11 and ∠5   _____   _____

13. ∠10 and ∠14   _____   _____

NAME _____

Check What You Know

Geometry

Write whether each triangle is acute, right, or obtuse and equilateral, isosceles, or scalene.

          a   b   c

14.

_____   _____   _____

Identify the following shapes. If more than one name applies, use the name that is most specific.

15.

_____   _____   _____

16.

_____   _____   _____

Use the grid at the right to answer the following.

17. What type of transformation is represented by figures *ABCDEFGH* and *IJKLMNOP*? _____

18. What is the ordered pair of Point *S*? _____

19. What is the ordered pair of Point *B*? _____

20. What point is at coordinates $(-3, -2)$? _____

21. What point is at coordinates $(1, 2)$? _____

22. In which quadrant is Point *T*? _____

23. Are the two figures in Quadrants I and II congruent? _____

Lesson 10.1　Points and Lines

A **point** is a location. It is represented by a dot. *Point R* is shown below.

•R

A **line** is a straight path that extends indefinitely in opposite directions. The line below could be identified as *Line ST, Line TS, $\overleftrightarrow{ST}$, or $\overleftrightarrow{TS}$.*

S　　T

A **line segment** is a straight path between two end points. The line segment below could be identified as *Line Segment UV, Line Segment VU, $\overline{UV}$, or $\overline{VU}$.*

U　　V

Complete the following.

		a	b
1.	R S	line　RS　or　SR	$\overleftrightarrow{RS}$　or　$\overleftrightarrow{SR}$
2.	P　Q	line _____ or _____	_____ or _____
3.	M　N	line _____ or _____	_____ or _____

		a	b	c
4.	X Y	line segment　XY　or ____	$\overline{XY}$　or ____	endpoints ____ and ____
5.	A　B	line segment ____ or ____	____ or ____	endpoints ____ and ____
6.	C D	line segment ____ or ____	____ or ____	endpoints ____ and ____

Draw the following.

　　　　　　　　　　a　　　　　　　　　　　　　　b

7. line *TU*　　　　　　　　　　　$\overleftrightarrow{OP}$

8. $\overline{GH}$　　　　　　　　　　　$\overleftrightarrow{JK}$

9. line segment *XY*　　　　　　　　$\overline{WX}$

Lesson 10.2 Rays and Angles

A **ray** is a part of a line. It has one endpoint and extends indefinitely in one direction. The ray below could be identified as *Ray RS* or $\overrightarrow{RS}$.

R •——————• S →

An **angle** is formed by two rays that intersect at a common endpoint. The angle below could be identified as *Angle ABC, Angle CBA*, $\angle ABC$, or $\angle CBA$.

The common endpoint of two rays is also called a **vertex**. In $\angle ABC$ to the left, the vertex is *B*.

Complete the following.

	a	**b**
1. A→B	ray *AB* $\overrightarrow{AB}$	endpoint *A*
2. C→D	ray _____ _____	endpoint _____
3. E→F	ray _____ _____	endpoint _____

4. angle *GHI* or *IHG* $\angle GHI$ or $\angle IHG$

rays: $\overrightarrow{HG}$ and $\overrightarrow{HI}$ vertex *H*

5. angle _____ or _____   _____ or _____

rays: _____ and _____   vertex _____

6. angle _____ or _____   _____ or _____

rays: _____ and _____   vertex _____

Use the points given to draw the following.

    a   **b**

7. $\overrightarrow{XY}$

8. $\angle RST$ $\angle PQR$

Lesson 10.3   Measuring Angles

Use a protractor to measure an angle.

The measure of a **right angle** is 90°.

The measure of an **acute angle** is less than 90°.

The measure of an **obtuse angle** is greater than 90°.

The measure of ∠XYZ is 50°.

right angle

This symbol means 90°.

obtuse angle

acute angle

Find the measure of each angle. Write whether the angle is right, acute, or obtuse.

a   b

1.

_____ _____   _____ _____

2.

_____ _____   _____ _____

3.

_____ _____   _____ _____

Lesson 10.4 Vertical, Supplementary, and Complementary Angles

When two lines intersect, they form angles that have special relationships.

Vertical angles are opposite angles that have the same measure.

Supplementary angles are two angles whose measures have a sum of 180°.

Complementary angles are two angles whose measures have a sum of 90°.

A **bisector** divides an angle into two angles of equal measure.

∠ABC and ∠DBE are vertical.

∠ABD and ∠DBE are supplementary.

∠WXZ and ∠ZXY are complementary.

$\overrightarrow{XZ}$ is the bisector of ∠WXY.

Use the figure at the right to answer questions 1–4.

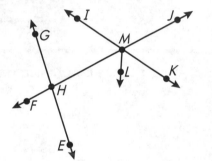

1. Name an angle that is vertical to ∠EHF. _____

2. Name an angle that is vertical to ∠EHM. _____

3. Name an angle that is supplementary to ∠IMJ. _____

4. Name the bisector of ∠HMK. _____

Use the figure at the right to answer questions 5 and 6.

5. Name an angle complementary to ∠BFC. _____

6. Name an angle complementary to ∠AFG. _____

Solve.

7. ∠RST is supplementary to angle ∠PSO. The measure of ∠RST is 103°.
   What is the measure of ∠PSO? _____

8. ∠MNO and ∠NOP are complementary. The measure of ∠NOP is 22°.
   What is the measure of ∠MNO? _____

9. ∠XYZ is bisected by $\overrightarrow{YW}$. The measure of ∠XYW is 52°.
   What is the measure of ∠WYZ? What is the measure of ∠XYZ?

   The measure of ∠WYZ is _____.   The measure of ∠XYZ is _____.

Lesson 10.5 Transversals

A **transversal** is a line that intersects two or more lines at different points. The angles that are formed are called **alternate interior angles** and **alternate exterior angles**. **Parallel lines** are lines that will never intersect. When a transversal intersects parallel lines, **corresponding angles** are formed.

In the figure, $\overleftrightarrow{ST}$ is a transversal. $\overleftrightarrow{WX}$ and $\overleftrightarrow{YZ}$ are parallel.

The alternate interior angles are $\angle 2$ and $\angle 8$, and $\angle 3$ and $\angle 5$.

The alternate exterior angles are $\angle 4$ and $\angle 6$, and $\angle 1$ and $\angle 7$.

The corresponding angles are $\angle 1$ and $\angle 5$, $\angle 2$ and $\angle 6$, $\angle 3$ and $\angle 7$, and $\angle 4$ and $\angle 8$.

Use the figure to the right. Name the transversal that forms each pair of angles. Write whether the angles are alternate interior, alternate exterior, or corresponding.

1. $\angle 1$ and $\angle 9$ _____ _____

2. $\angle 5$ and $\angle 4$ _____ _____

3. $\angle 11$ and $\angle 3$ _____ _____

4. $\angle 5$ and $\angle 16$ _____ _____

5. $\angle 13$ and $\angle 8$ _____ _____

6. $\angle 15$ and $\angle 10$ _____ _____

7. $\angle 7$ and $\angle 14$ _____ _____

8. $\angle 8$ and $\angle 16$ _____ _____

9. $\angle 6$ and $\angle 3$ _____ _____

10. $\angle 12$ and $\angle 13$ _____ _____

11. $\angle 10$ and $\angle 2$ _____ _____

12. $\angle 5$ and $\angle 13$ _____ _____

Lesson 10.6   Triangles (by angles)

The sum of the measures of the angles of a triangle is always 180°. Two of the angles are always acute. The triangle can be classified by the measure of the third angle as **right**, **acute**, or **obtuse**.

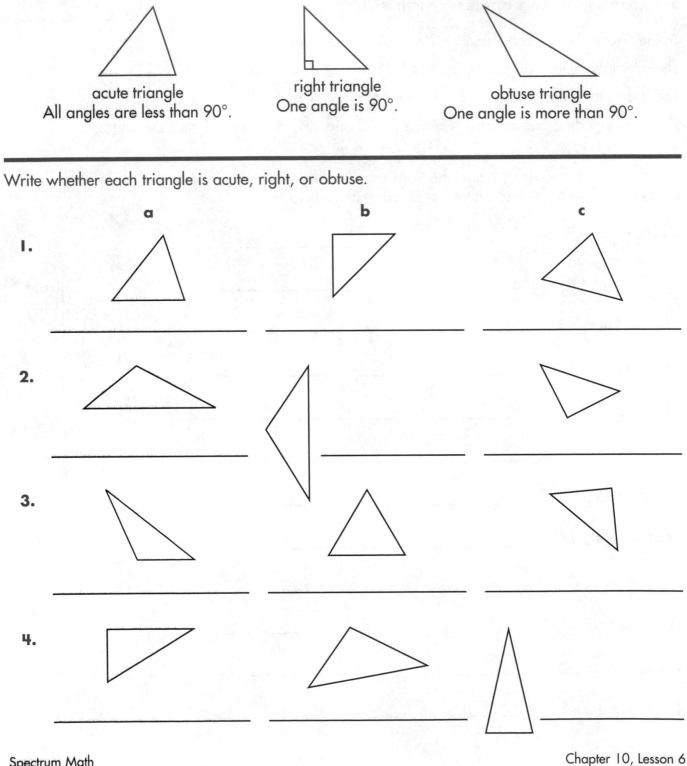

acute triangle
All angles are less than 90°.

right triangle
One angle is 90°.

obtuse triangle
One angle is more than 90°.

Write whether each triangle is acute, right, or obtuse.

	a	b	c
1.			
2.			
3.			
4.			

Lesson 10.7 Triangles (by side)

Triangles can be classified by the number of congruent (equal) sides that they have.

No two sides are congruent in a **scalene triangle**.

At least two sides are congruent in an **isosceles triangle**.

All three sides are congruent in an **equilateral triangle**.

equilateral   isosceles   scalene

Use a ruler to measure each triangle. Write if it is equilateral, isosceles, or scalene.

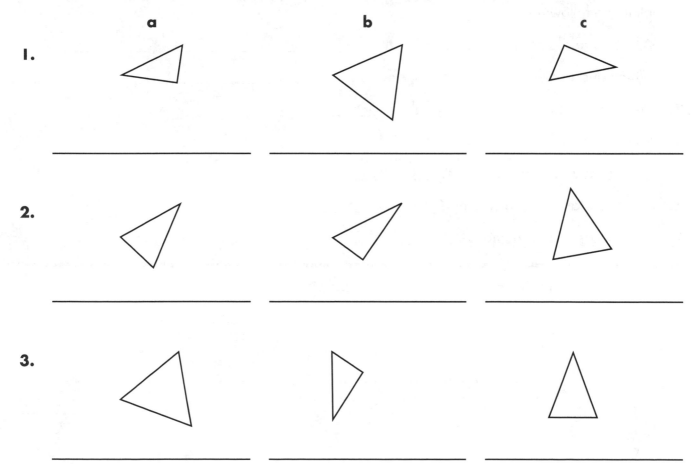

	a	b	c
1.			
2.			
3.			

Lesson 10.8   Quadrilaterals

A **quadrilateral** is a closed figure with 4 sides.

A **parallelogram** is a quadrilateral whose opposite sides are parallel and congruent.

A **rectangle** is a parallelogram with four right angles.

A **rhombus** is a parallelogram with four congruent sides.

A **square** has four right angles and four congruent sides.

A **trapezoid** is a quadrilateral with only one pair of parallel sides.

| parallelogram | rectangle | rhombus | square | trapezoid |

Complete the following.

1. Which quadrilaterals have four right angles? _____

2. Which quadrilaterals have four congruent sides? _____

3. Are all parallelograms also rectangles? _____

4. Are all rectangles also parallelograms? _____

5. Are all squares also rectangles? _____

6. Are all rectangles also squares? _____

7. Is a square also a rhombus? _____

Identify the following shapes. Use all terms that apply.

a   b

8. _____   _____

9. _____   _____

Lesson 10.9 Polygons

A **polygon** is a closed figure whose sides are all line segments. Polygons can be classified by the number of sides they have. The table shows some of the prefixes of polygons and the number of sides they represent.

Prefix	# of sides
penta-	5
hexa-	6
hepta-	7
octa-	8
nona-	9
deca-	10

pentagon
5 sides

octagon
8 sides

hexagon
6 sides

Write the name for each polygon.

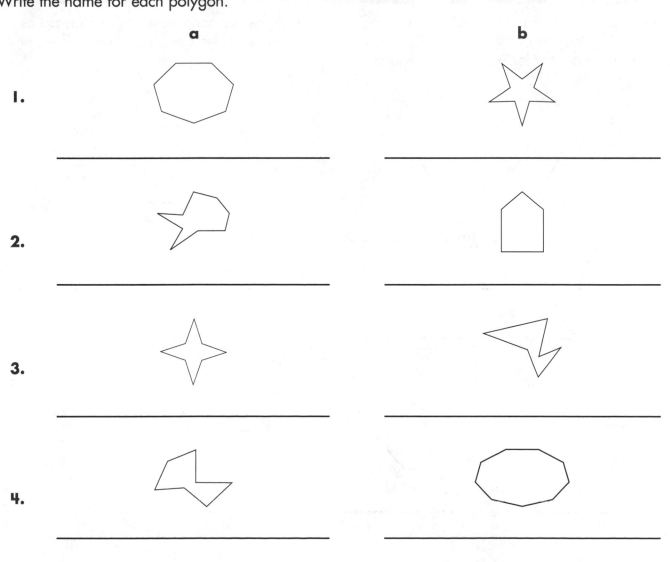

a

b

1.

2.

3.

4.

Lesson 10.10   Similar Figures

Two figures are **similar** if their corresponding angles are congruent and the lengths of their corresponding sides are proportional. Write a ratio to determine if the sides are proportional.

$\frac{AB}{SR} = \frac{BC}{ST}$? $\frac{1}{2} = \frac{2}{4}$ Similar

$\frac{AB}{WX} = \frac{BC}{XY}$? $\frac{1}{2} \neq \frac{2}{2}$ Not Similar

In the following figures, the angle marks indicate which angles are congruent. Use the measures given for the lengths of the sides. Write ratios to determine if the sides are proportional. Then, write *similar* or *not similar* for each pair of figures.

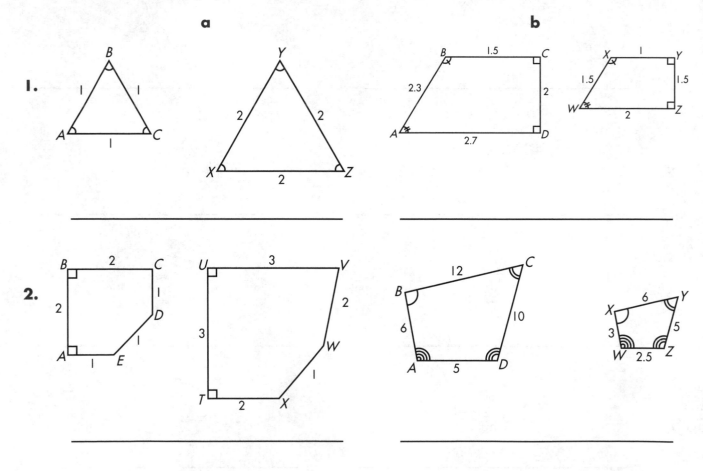

Lesson 10.11 Plotting Ordered Pairs

In a **coordinate plane**, the axes are labeled x and y. The coordinates of a point are represented by the ordered pair (x, y). The plane is divided into four quadrants, which are named in counterclockwise order. The signs on the ordered pairs in Quadrant I are (+, +), Quadrant II are (−, +), Quadrant III are (−, −) and Quadrant IV are (+, −).

Note: Before you complete this lesson, you may find it helpful to work through Lesson 12.7 *Adding and Subtracting Integers*.

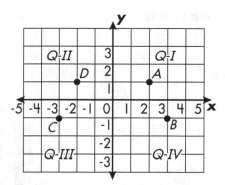

Point A has the coordinates (2, 1)
Point B has the coordinates (3, −1)
Point C has the coordinates (−3, −1)
Point D has the coordinates (−2, 1)

Use Grid 1 to name the point for each ordered pair.

	a		b	
1.	(2, 3) _____		(3, −1) _____	
2.	(−2, −2) _____		(−2, 3) _____	
3.	(1, −2) _____		(1, 1) _____	

Use Grid 2 to find the ordered pair for each point.

	a		b	
4.	A _____		F _____	
5.	B _____		G _____	
6.	C _____		H _____	

Plot the following points on Grid 3.

	a		b	
7.	A (2, 3)		D (2, −3)	
8.	B (−1, 4)		E (3, 2)	
9.	C (−2, −3)		F (−4, 2)	

Lesson 10.12 Transformations

A **transformation** is a change of the position or size of an image. In a **translation**, an image slides in any direction. In a **reflection**, an image is flipped over a line. In a **rotation**, an image is turned about a point. In a **dilation**, an image is enlarged or reduced. One way to view an image and its transformation is to graph it on a coordinate plane.

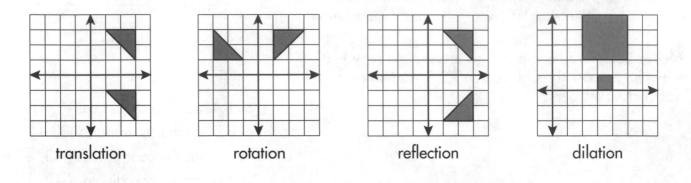

translation   rotation   reflection   dilation

Write whether each transformation is a translation, rotation, reflection, or dilation.

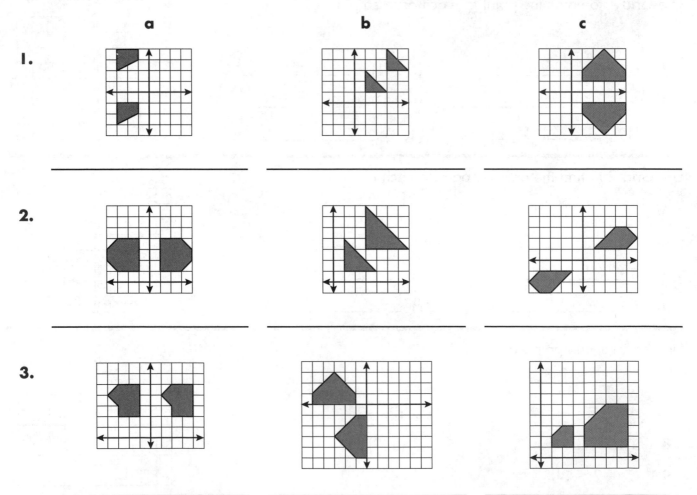

Check What You Learned

Geometry

Identify the following.

	a	**b**	**c**

1.

_____   _____   _____

2.

_____   _____   _____

Name the angle, rays, and vertex.

3.

angle: _____   rays: _____   vertex: _____

4.

angle: _____   rays: _____   vertex: _____

Use the figure to the right to complete the following.

5. What angle is vertical to ∠6? _____

6. What angle is supplementary to ∠11? _____

7. Which two lines are parallel? _____

8. If ∠11 is 70°, what is the measure of ∠10? _____

9. Is ∠10 acute, obtuse, or right? _____

Name the transversal that forms each pair of angles. Write whether the angles are alternate interior, alternate exterior, or corresponding.

10. ∠1 and ∠15   _____   _____

11. ∠6 and ∠10   _____   _____

12. ∠12 and ∠14   _____   _____

Check What You Learned

Geometry

Write whether each triangle is acute, right, or obtuse and equilateral, isosceles, or scalene.

a	b	c

13.

_____ _____ _____

Identify the following shapes. If more than one name applies, use the name that is most specific.

14.

_____ _____ _____

15.

_____ _____ _____

Use the grid at the right to answer the following.

16. What type of transformation is represented
by triangles *ABC* and *DEF*? _____

17. What type of transformation is represented
by triangles *DEF* and *GHI*? _____

18. What are the coordinates of Point *J*? _____

19. In which quadrant is Point *E*? _____

20. What point is at coordinates (−2, 3)? _____

21. What is the ordered pair of Point *A*? _____

22. Are triangles *ABC* and *GHI* similar? _____

If yes, write the ratios to show it. _____

Check What You Know

Perimeter, Area, and Volume

Find the perimeter of each figure.

a   **b**   **c**

1.

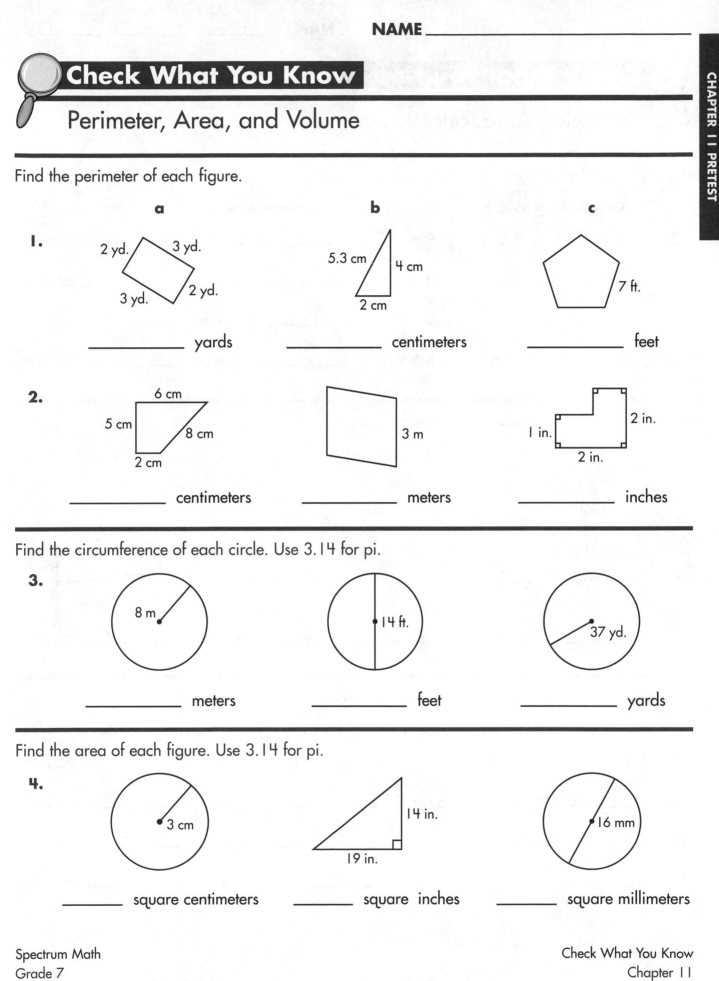

2 yd.   3 yd.
3 yd.   2 yd.

_____ yards

5.3 cm   4 cm
2 cm

_____ centimeters

7 ft.

_____ feet

2.

6 cm
5 cm
8 cm
2 cm

_____ centimeters

3 m

_____ meters

2 in.
1 in.
2 in.

_____ inches

Find the circumference of each circle. Use 3.14 for pi.

3.

8 m

_____ meters

14 ft.

_____ feet

37 yd.

_____ yards

Find the area of each figure. Use 3.14 for pi.

4.

3 cm

_____ square centimeters

14 in.
19 in.

_____ square inches

16 mm

_____ square millimeters

NAME _____

Check What You Know

Perimeter, Area, and Volume

Complete the table for each rectangular solid.

	Length	Width	Height	Surface Area	Volume
5.	4 m	2 m	9 m	_____ sq. m	_____ cubic m
6.	14 in.	9 in.	3 in.	_____ sq. in.	_____ cubic in.
7.	8.5 cm	4 cm	2.5 cm	_____ sq. cm	_____ cubic cm
8.	32 ft.	11 ft.	8.5 ft.	_____ sq. ft.	_____ cubic ft.

Find the volume for each triangular solid.

	a	b	c
9.	9 ft. / 7 ft. / 8 ft.	12 m / 15 m / 4 m	2.5 yd. / 5 yd. / 4 yd.
	_____ cubic feet	_____ cubic meters	_____ cubic yards

Complete the table for each cylinder. Use 3.14 for pi.

	Radius	Diameter	Height	Surface Area	Volume
10.	3 ft.	_____ ft.	11 ft.	_____ sq. ft.	_____ cubic ft.
11.	_____ cm	18 cm	5 cm	_____ sq. cm	_____ cubic cm
12.	2.5 m	_____ m	16 m	_____ sq. m	_____ cubic m
13.	_____ in.	38 in.	32 in.	_____ sq. in.	_____ cubic in.

Lesson 11.1   Perimeter

The **perimeter** of a figure is the sum of the lengths of its sides. If two or more sides are equal, the formula can be simplified with multiplication.

triangle	rectangle	square
$p = a + b + c$	$p = \ell + \ell + w + w$	$p = s + s + s + s$
	$p = 2\ell + 2w$	$p = 4s$

In the rectangle above, if the length is 6 cm and the width is 2 cm, the perimeter is
$2(6) + 2(2) = 12 + 4 = 16$ cm.

Find the perimeter of each figure.

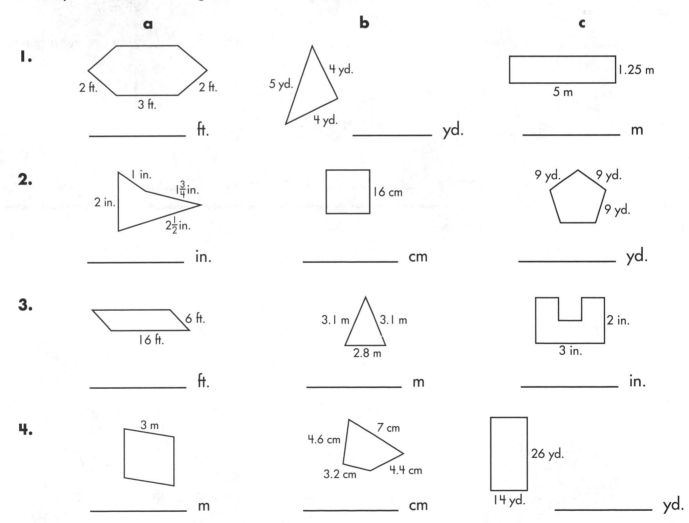

a   **b**   **c**

1.

_____ ft.   _____ yd.   _____ m

2.

_____ in.   _____ cm   _____ yd.

3.

_____ ft.   _____ m   _____ in.

4.

_____ m   _____ cm   _____ yd.

Lesson 11.2 Area of Rectangles

Area is the number of square units it takes to cover a figure. To find the area of a rectangle, multiply the length by the width.

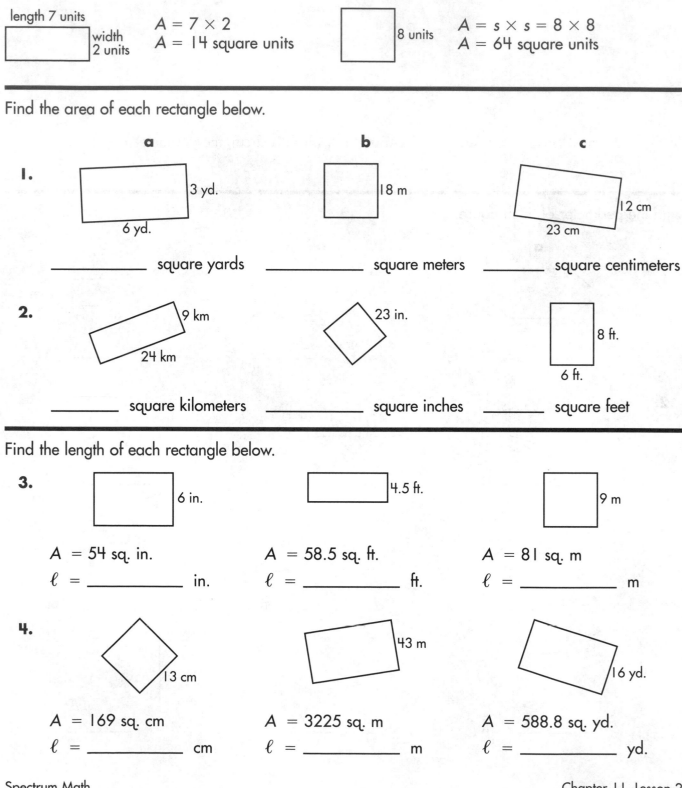

length 7 units

width 2 units

$A = 7 \times 2$
$A = 14$ square units

8 units

$A = s \times s = 8 \times 8$
$A = 64$ square units

Find the area of each rectangle below.

	a	**b**	**c**

1.

3 yd.
6 yd.

18 m

12 cm
23 cm

_____ square yards   _____ square meters   _____ square centimeters

2.

9 km
24 km

23 in.

8 ft.
6 ft.

_____ square kilometers   _____ square inches   _____ square feet

Find the length of each rectangle below.

3.

6 in.

4.5 ft.

9 m

$A = 54$ sq. in.
$\ell = $ _____ in.

$A = 58.5$ sq. ft.
$\ell = $ _____ ft.

$A = 81$ sq. m
$\ell = $ _____ m

4.

13 cm

43 m

16 yd.

$A = 169$ sq. cm
$\ell = $ _____ cm

$A = 3225$ sq. m
$\ell = $ _____ m

$A = 588.8$ sq. yd.
$\ell = $ _____ yd.

Lesson 11.3 Area of Triangles

The area of a triangle is the product of $\frac{1}{2}$ of the base times the height. It is related to the area of a rectangle.

The dashed line indicates the height of the triangle.

rectangle: $A = 8 \times 6 = 48$ sq. units

triangle: $A = \frac{1}{2}(8)(6) = 24$ sq. units

$A = \frac{1}{2}(4.5)(3) = 6\frac{3}{4}$ sq. m

Notice that in a right triangle the height is the length of one of the legs. This is not the case with acute and obtuse triangles.

Find the area of each triangle below.

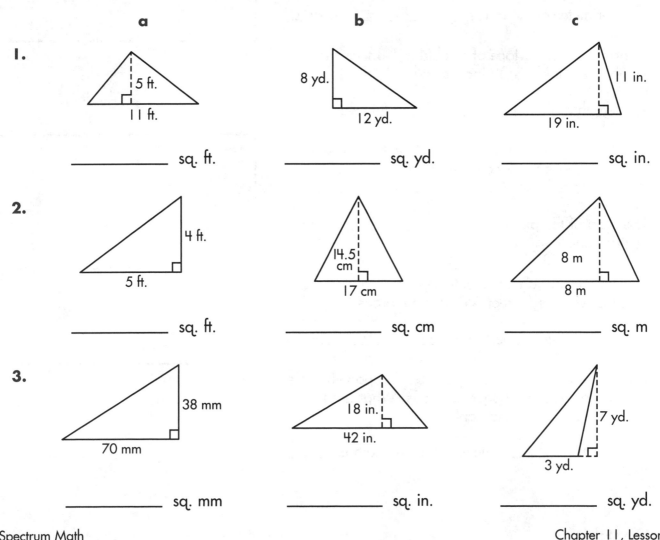

	a	b	c
1.	5 ft. / 11 ft.	8 yd. / 12 yd.	11 in. / 19 in.
	_____ sq. ft.	_____ sq. yd.	_____ sq. in.
2.	4 ft. / 5 ft.	14.5 cm / 17 cm	8 m / 8 m
	_____ sq. ft.	_____ sq. cm	_____ sq. m
3.	38 mm / 70 mm	18 in. / 42 in.	7 yd. / 3 yd.
	_____ sq. mm	_____ sq. in.	_____ sq. yd.

Lesson 11.4   Problem Solving

Solve each problem.

1. The Robinsons want to put a fence around part of their yard. The width of the area is 22 feet and the length is 47 feet. What is the length of fence they will need?

   They will need _____ feet of fence.

   1.

2. Alicia made lasagna in a pan measuring 12 inches by 9 inches. What is the area of the lasagna?

   The area of the lasagna is _____ square inches.

   2.

3. Akira planted a garden in the shape of a triangle. The lengths of the sides of the garden are 3 meters, 4 meters, and 5 meters. What is the perimeter?

   The perimeter of the garden is _____ meters.

   3.

4. The area of the surface of a table is 1,836 inches. The width of the table is 34 inches. What is the length?

   The length of the table is _____ inches.

   4.

5. Josie is using a triangular piece of cloth to make a scarf. The base is 62 centimeters and the height is 41 centimeters. What is the area of the cloth?

   The area of the piece of cloth is _____ square centimeters.

   5.

6. Becky is buying a new countertop. The length is $4\frac{1}{4}$ feet and the width is $2\frac{1}{2}$ feet. What is the area?

   The area of the countertop is _____ square feet.

   6.

7. Rob made brownies in a square baking pan. The area of the brownies is 64 square inches. What are the length and width of the pan?

   The length is _____ inches and the width is _____ inches.

   7.

Lesson 11.5   Circumference of Circles

A **circle** is a set of points that are all the same distance from a given point, called the **center**. The perimeter of a circle is called the **circumference**. The **diameter** is a segment that passes through the center of the circle and has both endpoints on the circle. The **radius** is a segment that has as its endpoints the circle and the center. The relationship between the circumference (C) and the diameter (d) is C ÷ d = π. Pi (π) is approximately $3\frac{1}{7}$ or 3.14. To find the circumference, diameter, or radius of a circle, use the formulas C = π × d or C = 2 × π × r.

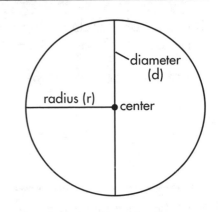

Complete the table. Use 3.14 for pi.

	a Diameter	b Radius	c Circumference
1.	_____ feet	_____ feet	4.71 feet
2.	3.5 meters	_____ meters	_____ meters
3.	_____ inches	3.25 inches	_____ inches
4.	_____ yards	_____ yards	26.69 yards
5.	7.5 centimeters	_____ centimeters	_____ centimeters
6.	_____ inches	15 inches	_____ inches
7.	_____ meters	_____ meters	7.85 meters
8.	5 kilometers	_____ kilometers	_____ kilometers
9.	_____ feet	_____ feet	31.4 feet
10.	_____ centimeters	45 centimeters	_____ centimeters
11.	4 yards	_____ yards	_____ yards
12.	_____ miles	_____ miles	9.42 miles

Lesson 11.6   Area of Circles

The area of a circle is found by using the formula $A = \pi \times r \times r$. Remember, π can be expressed as $3\frac{1}{7}$ or as 3.14. If you know the diameter of a circle, divide by 2 to find the radius.

What is the area if $r = 6$?

$A = \frac{22}{7}(6)(6)$

$A = 113\frac{1}{7}$ square units

What is the area if $d = 8$?

$A = 3.14 \times \frac{8}{2} \times \frac{8}{2}$

$A = 3.14 \times 4 \times 4$

$A = 50.24$ square units

Find the area of each circle below. Use 3.14 for pi. Round your answer to the nearest tenth.

| | a | b | c |

1.

_____ square feet   _____ square meters   _____ square centimeters

8 ft.   12 m   13 cm

2.

_____ square yards   _____ square kilometers   _____ square inches

36 yd.   12 km   7 in.

Complete the table. Use 3.14 for pi. Round your answer to the nearest tenth.

	Diameter	Radius	Area
3.	_____ inches	3 inches	_____ square inches
4.	18 feet	_____ feet	_____ square feet
5.	17 meters	_____ meters	_____ square meters
6.	_____ centimeters	32 centimeters	_____ square centimeters
7.	30 kilometers	_____ kilometers	_____ square kilometers
8.	_____ yards	6 yards	_____ square yards

Lesson 11.7 Area of Irregular Shapes

To find the area of irregular shapes, separate the shapes into figures for which you can find the area.

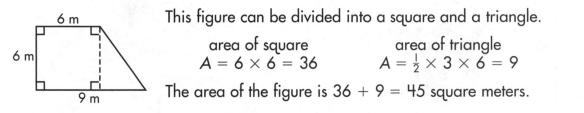

This figure can be divided into a square and a triangle.

area of square	area of triangle
$A = 6 \times 6 = 36$	$A = \frac{1}{2} \times 3 \times 6 = 9$

The area of the figure is $36 + 9 = 45$ square meters.

Find the area of each figure.

        a   b   c

1.

_____ square feet   _____ square meters   _____ square centimeters

2.

_____ square yards

_____ square miles

_____ square inches

3.

_____ square feet

_____ square inches

_____ square centimeters

Lesson 11.8 Surface Area (Rectangular Solids)

The **surface area** of a solid is the sum of the areas of all the faces (or surfaces of the solid). The surface area of a rectangular solid can be found by the formula $SA = 2\ell w + 2\ell h + 2wh$.

$SA = 2(1.5)(1.2) + 2(1.5)(1.6) + 2(1.2)(1.6)$

$SA = 3.6 \qquad\quad + 4.8 \qquad\quad + 3.84$

$SA = 12.24$ square feet

1.6 ft.   1.2 ft.   1.5 ft.

Find the surface area of each figure.

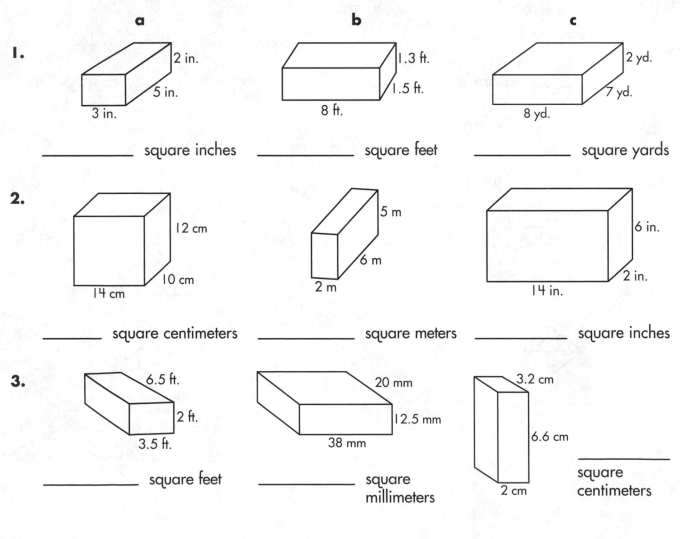

           a   **b**   **c**

1.   2 in. / 5 in. / 3 in.   1.3 ft. / 1.5 ft. / 8 ft.   2 yd. / 7 yd. / 8 yd.

_____ square inches   _____ square feet   _____ square yards

2.   12 cm / 10 cm / 14 cm   5 m / 6 m / 2 m   6 in. / 2 in. / 14 in.

_____ square centimeters   _____ square meters   _____ square inches

3.   6.5 ft. / 2 ft. / 3.5 ft.   20 mm / 12.5 mm / 38 mm   3.2 cm / 6.6 cm / 2 cm

_____ square feet   _____ square millimeters   _____ square centimeters

Lesson 11.9 Volume of Rectangular Solids

The **volume** of a rectangular solid is the product of the length times width times height. The product of the length times width is the base. The formula for the volume is $V = B \times h$. Volume is expressed in cubic units.

$B = 3 \times 2 = 6$

$V = B \times h = 6 \times 3.5$

$V = 21$ cubic meters

Find the volume of each figure.

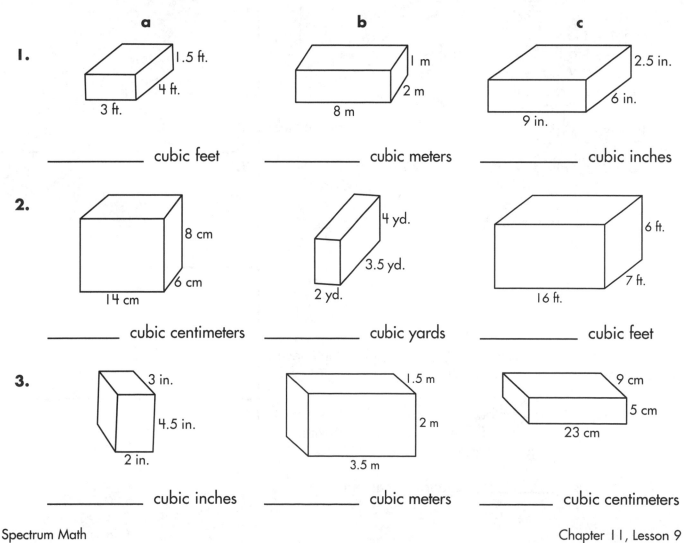

	a	b	c
1.	1.5 ft. / 4 ft. / 3 ft.	1 m / 2 m / 8 m	2.5 in. / 6 in. / 9 in.
	_____ cubic feet	_____ cubic meters	_____ cubic inches
2.	8 cm / 6 cm / 14 cm	4 yd. / 3.5 yd. / 2 yd.	6 ft. / 7 ft. / 16 ft.
	_____ cubic centimeters	_____ cubic yards	_____ cubic feet
3.	3 in. / 4.5 in. / 2 in.	1.5 m / 2 m / 3.5 m	9 cm / 5 cm / 23 cm
	_____ cubic inches	_____ cubic meters	_____ cubic centimeters

Lesson 11.10 Problem Solving

Solve each problem.

1. The radius of a glass is 1.25 inches. What is the circumference? Use 3.14 for pi.

    The circumference of the glass is _____ inches.

2. Juan left a garbage can on the lawn, and the grass underneath it died. The diameter of the can is 54 centimeters. What is the area of the grass that died? Use 3.14 for pi.

    The area of the grass is _____ square centimeters.

3. A drawing of a house is made up of a rectangle for the walls and a triangle for the roof. The base of the drawing is 9 inches wide. The height of the walls is 7 inches. And the height to the top of the roof is 10 inches. What is the area of the house in the drawing?

    10 in.   7 in.

    9 in.

    The area of the drawing is _____ square inches.

4. A building with a flat roof is 11 meters long, 8 meters wide, and 6 meters high. What is the surface area?

    The surface area of the building is _____ square meters.

5. An aquarium is 50 centimeters long, 20 centimeters wide, and 30 centimeters high. How many cubic centimeters of water can it hold?

    The aquarium can hold _____ cubic centimeters of water.

6. Opal needs to wrap a box. The box is 12 inches by 8 inches by 1.5 inches. If she wants to wrap it with no overlap, how much paper does she need?

    Opal needs _____ square inches of paper.

1.

2.

3.

4.

5.

6.

Lesson 11.11 Volume of Triangular Solids

The bases of a triangular solid are triangles. To find the volume, multiply the area of one base times the height.

$B = \frac{1}{2}bh = \frac{1}{2}(9)(2) = 9$

$V = B \times h$

$V = 9 \times 5$

$V = 45$ cubic centimeters

Find the volume of each figure.

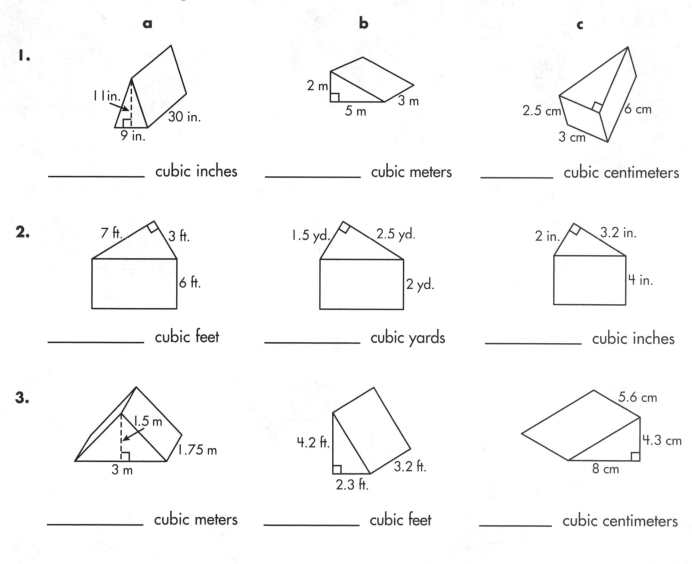

	a	b	c

1.

a: 11 in., 30 in., 9 in. — _____ cubic inches

b: 2 m, 5 m, 3 m — _____ cubic meters

c: 2.5 cm, 6 cm, 3 cm — _____ cubic centimeters

2.

a: 7 ft., 3 ft., 6 ft. — _____ cubic feet

b: 1.5 yd., 2.5 yd., 2 yd. — _____ cubic yards

c: 2 in., 3.2 in., 4 in. — _____ cubic inches

3.

a: 1.5 m, 1.75 m, 3 m — _____ cubic meters

b: 4.2 ft., 3.2 ft., 2.3 ft. — _____ cubic feet

c: 5.6 cm, 4.3 cm, 8 cm — _____ cubic centimeters

Lesson 11.12   Surface Area (Cylinders)

A cylinder can be represented on a flat surface as two circles for the bases and a rectangle. The height of the cylinder is the width of the rectangle. The circumference of the base is the length. The surface area is the sum of the area of these three surfaces. It is found by the formula $2\pi r^2 + 2\pi rh$.

$SA = 2(3.14)(8)(8) + 2(3.14)(8)(30)$

$SA = 401.92 \qquad + 1507.2$

$SA = 1909.12$ square centimeters

8 cm

30 cm

Find the surface area of each cylinder. Use 3.14 for π.

a   **b**   **c**

1.

12 in.   4 in.   22 ft.   6 ft.   13 mm   51 mm

_____ square inches   _____ square feet   _____ square millimeters

2.

3 yd.   2.5 yd.   5 cm   14 cm   8 ft.   12 ft.

_____ square yards   _____ square centimeters   _____ square feet

3.

3 m   6.2 m   7 in.   18 in.   14 cm   48 cm

_____ square meters   _____ square inches   _____ square centimeters

Lesson 11.13 Volume of Cylinders

The volume of a cylinder is the product of the area of the base *(B)* times the height. The formula for the volume of a cylinder is $V = B \times h$.

$B = \pi r^2 = (3.14)(8)(8) = 200.96$

$V = 200.96 \times 10$

$V = 2009.6$ cubic feet

8 ft.

10 ft.

Find the volume of each cylinder. Use 3.14 for π.

	a	**b**	**c**
1.	16 in. / 20 in.	23 cm / 14 cm	6.3 ft. / 6 ft.
	_____ cubic inches	_____ cubic centimeters	_____ cubic feet
2.	12 m / 14 m	8 mm / 42 mm	2 in. / 7 in.
	_____ cubic meters	_____ cubic millimeters	_____ cubic inches
3.	64.2 mm / 23 mm	18 yd. / 2 yd.	8.6 cm / 21 cm
	_____ cubic millimeters	_____ cubic yards	_____ cubic centimeters

Lesson 11.14 Problem Solving

SHOW YOUR WORK

Solve each problem.

1. When a certain tent is pitched, it forms a triangular pyramid. It is 2 meters high. The width is 3 meters, and the length is 4.5 meters. What is the volume of the tent?

   2 m 4.5 m 3 m

   The volume of the tent is _____ cubic meters.

   1.

2. A triangular wedge of cheese has the dimensions shown in the figure. What is the volume?

   10 cm 2 cm 4 cm

   The volume of the cheese is _____ cubic centimeters.

   2.

3. A wooden block is cut in the shape of a triangular solid. Its volume is 3 cubic inches and the area of its base is 1.5 square inches. What is its height?

   The block is _____ inches high.

   3.

4. A peanut butter jar is 16.5 centimeters tall and has a diameter of 9 centimeters. What is its surface area? What is its volume?

   The surface area of the jar is _____ square centimeters.

   The volume of the jar is _____ cubic centimeters.

   4.

5. A can of paint is 8 inches high and has a radius of 3.5 inches. What is its surface area? What is its volume?

   The surface area of the can is _____ square inches.

   The volume of the can is _____ cubic inches.

   5.

6. A holding tank in a manufacturing plant is 6.3 meters tall and has a diameter of 4 meters. What is its surface area? What is its volume?

   The surface area of the tank is _____ square meters.

   The volume of the tank is _____ cubic meters.

   6.

Check What You Learned

Perimeter, Area, and Volume

Find the perimeter of each figure.

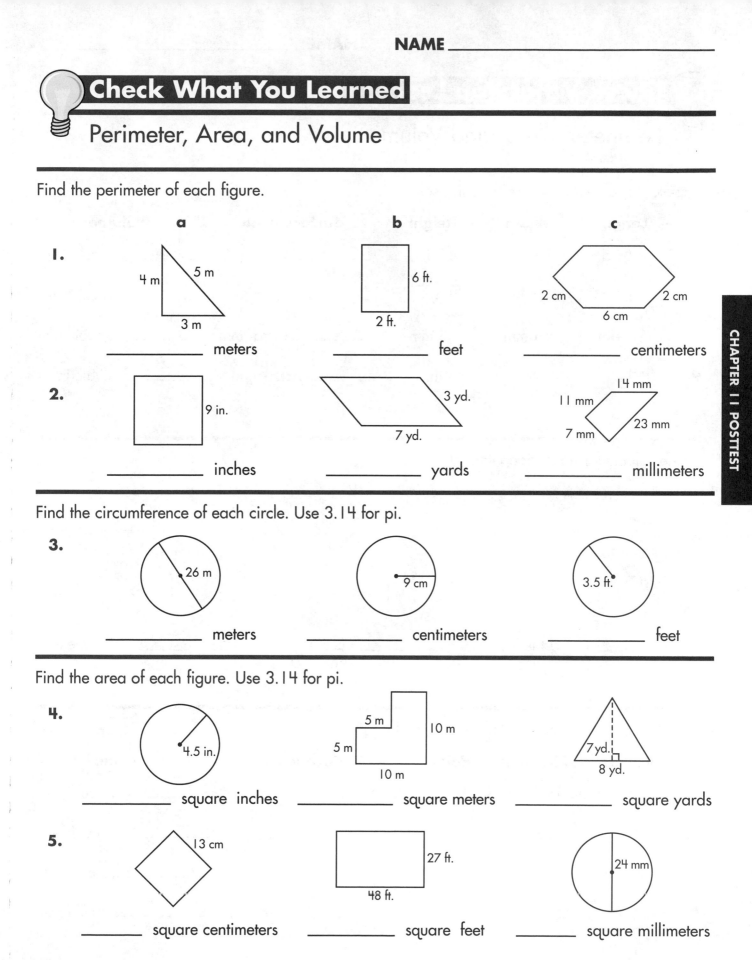

	a	b	c
1.	5 m, 4 m, 3 m	6 ft., 2 ft.	2 cm, 2 cm, 6 cm
	_____ meters	_____ feet	_____ centimeters
2.	9 in.	3 yd., 7 yd.	14 mm, 11 mm, 23 mm, 7 mm
	_____ inches	_____ yards	_____ millimeters

Find the circumference of each circle. Use 3.14 for pi.

3.

26 m

_____ meters

9 cm

_____ centimeters

3.5 ft.

_____ feet

Find the area of each figure. Use 3.14 for pi.

4.

4.5 in.

_____ square inches

5 m, 10 m, 5 m, 10 m

_____ square meters

7 yd., 8 yd.

_____ square yards

5.

13 cm

_____ square centimeters

27 ft., 48 ft.

_____ square feet

24 mm

_____ square millimeters

Check What You Learned

Perimeter, Area, and Volume

Complete the table for each rectangular solid.

	Length	Width	Height	Surface Area	Volume
6.	4.5 yd.	2 yd.	8 yd.	_____ sq. yd.	_____ cubic yd.
7.	3 m	1.5 m	4 m	_____ sq. m	_____ cubic m
8.	23 mm	14 mm	18 mm	_____ sq. mm	_____ cubic mm
9.	5 in.	1.5 in.	6 in.	_____ sq. in.	_____ cubic in.

Find the volume for each triangular solid.

a	b	c

10.

_____ cubic inches   _____ cubic centimeters   _____ cubic meters

Complete the table for each cylinder. Use 3.14 for pi.

	Radius	Diameter	Height	Surface Area	Volume
11.	_____ m	3 m	8 m	_____ sq. m	_____ cubic m
12.	2 yd.	_____ yd.	7 yd.	_____ sq. yd.	_____ cubic yd.
13.	_____ in.	22 in.	34 in.	_____ sq. in.	_____ cubic in.
14.	7 cm	_____ cm	3 cm	_____ sq. cm	_____ cubic cm

Check What You Know

Preparing for Algebra

Write each phrase as a variable expression.

| | **a** | **b** |

1. five less than n

_____

eight more than b

_____

2. a number divided by six

_____

the product of two and a number

_____

Write each sentence as an equation.

3. The sum of three and a number is twelve.

_____

Six less than x is nineteen.

_____

4. Thirty divided by a number is three.

_____

The product of five and n is fifteen.

_____

Solve each equation.

	a	**b**	**c**
5.	$8 + d = 14$ _____	$s + 3 = 12$ _____	$9 + c = 21$ _____
6.	$25 = 10 + a$ _____	$13 = 9 + b$ _____	$26 = 4 + n$ _____
7.	$18 - x = 4$ _____	$31 - n = 19$ _____	$17 - b = 1$ _____
8.	$7 = 24 - y$ _____	$11 = 15 - b$ _____	$23 = 23 - n$ _____
9.	$3 \times a = 15$ _____	$2 \times n = 12$ _____	$5 \times d = 35$ _____
10.	$27 = 9 \times b$ _____	$24 = 6 \times n$ _____	$42 = 7 \times b$ _____
11.	$n \div 9 = 4$ _____	$b \div 6 = 7$ _____	$d \div 7 = 2$ _____
12.	$6 = b \div 3$ _____	$3 = a \div 20$ _____	$8 = c \div 9$ _____

NAME _____

Check What You Know

Preparing for Algebra

Find the value of each expression. Round to five decimal places if necessary.

	a	b	c
13.	$20 \div (5 - 1) =$ _____	$3 \times (6 + 2) =$ _____	$2 + 3 \times 6 =$ _____
14.	$9 + 2 - 3 =$ _____	$4 + (16 \div 4) =$ _____	$(4 + 16) \div 4 =$ _____
15.	$-3 + 2 =$ _____	$3 + (-2) =$ _____	$7 + (-4) =$ _____
16.	$-8 + (-3) =$ _____	$-7 + 6 =$ _____	$-4 + (-9) =$ _____
17.	$6 - 12 =$ _____	$3 - (-4) =$ _____	$-2 - 4 =$ _____
18.	$-8 - (-3) =$ _____	$7 - (-2) =$ _____	$-6 - (-5) =$ _____
19.	$7 \times (-6) =$ _____	$3 \times (-4) =$ _____	$-5 \times (-2) =$ _____
20.	$-4 \times 5 =$ _____	$-8 \times (-2) =$ _____	$6 \times (-4) =$ _____
21.	$12 \div (-4) =$ _____	$-15 \div (-5) =$ _____	$-21 \div 7 =$ _____
22.	$-24 \div (-8) =$ _____	$20 \div (-4) =$ _____	$6 \div (-2) =$ _____
23.	$3^2 \times 3^3 =$ _____	$2^2 \times 2^4 =$ _____	$4^2 \times 4^1 =$ _____
24.	$5^4 \div 5^2 =$ _____	$8^6 \div 8^4 =$ _____	$4^5 \times 4 =$ _____
25.	$2^{-2} \times 2^{-2} =$ _____	$3^{-3} \times 3^2 =$ _____	$5^{-3} \times 5^{-1} =$ _____
26.	$3^{-4} \div 3^{-2} =$ _____	$6^{-3} \div 6^2 =$ _____	$2^{-5} \div 2^{-3} =$ _____

Lesson 12.1 Variables, Expressions, and Equations

An **expression** is a way of naming a number.

A **numerical expression** contains only numbers.	$2 + 5$
A **variable expression** contains numbers and variables.	$2 + c$
An **equation** is a mathematical sentence that states that two expressions are equal.	$2 + 5 = 7$ $2 + c = 7$
An **inequality** is a mathematical sentence that states that two expressions are not equal.	$2 + 5 > 6$ $2 + 5 < 9$

Write whether each of the following is a numerical expression, a variable expression, an equation, or an inequality.

	a	b	c
1.	$r - 17$	$b + 12 = 15$	$s - 11 < 52$
	_____	_____	_____
2.	12×3	$15 - 9 > y$	$47 - 19 = 28$
	_____	_____	_____

Write each phrase as a numerical or variable expression.

	a	b
3.	three more than d _____	the product of eight and w _____
4.	seven less than twelve _____	two more than a number _____
5.	a number divided by six _____	nine more than fifteen _____

Write each sentence as an equation or inequality.

6. The sum of five and six is eleven.

_____

Twelve divided by s equals 4.

_____

7. Three less than t is greater than five.

_____

The product of two and b is greater than four.

_____

8. The product of five and three is y.

_____

Twenty divided by a number is five.

_____

Lesson 12.2 Number Properties

Commutative Property: The order in which numbers are added $a + b = b + a$
does not change the sum. The order in which numbers are multiplied $a \times b = b \times a$
does not change the product.

Associative Property: The grouping of addends does not $a + (b + c) = (a + b) + c$
change the sum. The grouping of factors does not change the $a \times (b \times c) = (a \times b) \times c$
product.

Identity Property: The sum of an addend and 0 is the addend. $a + 0 = a$
The product of a factor and 1 is the factor. $a \times 1 = a$

Properties of Zero: The product of a factor and 0 is 0. The $a \times 0 = 0$
quotient of the dividend 0 and any divisor is 0. $0 \div a = 0$

Write the name of the property shown by each equation.

a

b

1. $3 + s = s + 3$ _____ $3 \times (2 \times r) = (3 \times 2) \times r$ _____

2. $15 \times 1 = 15$ _____ $12 \times p = p \times 12$ _____

3. $(6+t)+37 = 6+(t+37)$ _____ $35 \times 0 = 0$ _____

4. $346 + 0 = 346$ _____ $65 + 93 = 93 + 65$ _____

5. $0 \div 76 = 0$ _____ $(8 \times 9) \times 12 = 8 \times (9 \times 12)$ _____

Rewrite each expression using the property indicated.

6. associative: $(3 + 7) + y =$ _____   identity: $642 + 0 =$ _____

7. commutative: $15 \times z =$ _____   zero: $16 \times 0 =$ _____

8. identity: $12a \times 1 =$ _____   associative: $14 \times (3 \times p) =$ _____

9. zero: $0 \div 68 =$ _____   commutative: $49 + 16 =$ _____

10. commutative: $3 + d =$ _____   associative: $(6 \times 4) \times n =$ _____

Lesson 12.3 The Distributive Property

The **distributive property** combines multiplication with addition or subtraction. The property states:

$$a \times (b + c) = (a \times b) + (a \times c)$$
$$a \times (b - c) = (a \times b) - (a \times c)$$

$$3 \times (6 + 4) = (3 \times 6) + (3 \times 4)$$
$$3 \times (10) = (18) + (12)$$
$$30 = 30$$

Rewrite each expression using the distributive property.

a	**b**
1. $(a \times 4) + (a \times 3) =$	$b \times (6 + 12) =$
2. $4 \times (a + b) =$	$(3 \times a) + (3 \times b) =$
3. $(d \times 5) - (d \times 2) =$	$5 \times (8 + p) =$
4. $d \times (8 - h) =$	$12 \times (s - 10) =$
5. $r \times (16 + s) =$	$(35 \times t) + (35 \times y) =$
6. $(8 \times a) + (b \times 8) =$	$r \times (q - s) =$
7. $(6 \times 12) - (w \times 6) =$	$p \times (15 + z) =$
8. $15 \times (y + 0) =$	$(d \times d) + (d \times b) =$
9. $(a \times 2) + (a \times 3) + (a \times 4) =$	$p \times (a + b + 4) =$
10. $(a \times b) + (a \times c) - (a \times d) =$	$8 \times (a + b + c) =$

Lesson 12.4 Order of Operations

If an expression contains two or more operations, they must be completed in a specified order. The order of operations is as follows.

1. Complete operations within grouping symbols, such as parentheses.

2. Multiply and divide in order from left to right.

3. Add and subtract in order from left to right.

$$23 - (2 + 3) \times 2 = 23 - 5 \times 2 \qquad \text{Add } (2 + 3).$$
$$= 23 - 10 \qquad \text{Multiply } 5 \times 2.$$
$$= 13 \qquad \text{Subtract } 23 - 10.$$

Find the value of each expression.

	a	b	c
1.	$6 + 2 \times 5 =$ _____	$18 - (3 + 4) =$ _____	$18 - 3 + 4 =$ _____
2.	$3 \times 3 + 8 =$ _____	$3 \times (3 + 8) =$ _____	$12 \div (2 \times 3) =$ _____
3.	$12 \div 2 + 3 =$ _____	$8 + (5 \times 4) =$ _____	$8 + 5 \times 4 =$ _____
4.	$3 \times (2 \times 6) =$ _____	$15 \div (3 + 2) =$ _____	$15 \div 3 + 2 =$ _____
5.	$12 + 8 - 6 =$ _____	$2 + 6 \div 2 =$ _____	$(2 + 6) \div 2 =$ _____
6.	$3 \times 2 \div 6 =$ _____	$6 \div 3 \times 2 =$ _____	$8 - (2 + 4) =$ _____
7.	$30 \div 5 + 1 =$ _____	$30 \div (5 + 1) =$ _____	$7 + 12 \div 4 =$ _____
8.	$23 - 15 \div 3 =$ _____	$(32 - 7) \div 5 =$ _____	$48 - (12 \div 4) =$ _____
9.	$2 + 2 \times 3 - 1 =$ _____	$(2 + 2) \times 3 - 1 =$ _____	$3 + 4 \times 3 + 2 =$ _____
10.	$3 + 8 \div 2 - 1 =$ _____	$(4 + 8) \div (5 - 1) =$ _____	$12 \div (2 + 2) + 2 =$ _____
11.	$9 + 18 \div 6 - 3 =$ _____	$(9 + 18) \div (6 - 3) =$ _____	$3 + 2 \times 8 \div 4 =$ _____
12.	$10 - 8 \times 3 \div 6 =$ _____	$3 + 6 + 9 \div 3 =$ _____	$3 + (6 + 9) \div 3 =$ _____
13.	$12 - 10 + 2 \times 7 =$ _____	$(4 \times 3) + (4 \times 5) =$ _____	$4 \times (3 + 4) \times 5 =$ _____
14.	$8 + 2 \times 5 - 7 =$ _____	$(8 + 2) \times 5 - 7 =$ _____	$12 + 3 \times 10 \div 6 =$ _____

Lesson 12.5 Solving Addition and Subtraction Equations

Subtraction Property of Equality: When two expressions are equal,
if you subtract the same number from both expressions, the differences will
also be equal.

$a = b$
$a - c = b - c$

Addition Property of Equality: When two expressions are equal, if
you add the same number to both expressions, the sums will also be equal.

$a = b$
$a + c = b + c$

Use these properties to solve equations.

$a + 3 = 14$ $b - 11 = 6$

$a + 3 - 3 = 14 - 3$ $b - 11 + 11 = 6 + 11$

$a = 11$ $b = 17$

Solve each equation.

a	**b**	**c**
1. $9 + d = 16$ _____	$y + 3 = 9$ _____	$12 + a = 27$ _____
2. $18 - b = 4$ _____	$23 - c = 21$ _____	$w - 11 = 11$ _____
3. $n + 8 = 41$ _____	$7 + m = 20$ _____	$9 + s = 9$ _____
4. $t - 18 = 5$ _____	$36 - a = 36$ _____	$15 - b = 0$ _____
5. $17 = c + 3$ _____	$29 = 5 + b$ _____	$36 = 35 + n$ _____
6. $2 = d - 4$ _____	$19 = 25 - a$ _____	$12 = t - 12$ _____

Write an equation for each problem. Then, solve the equation.

7. Ruben read 37 pages in his history book over the weekend. He read 21 pages on Saturday. How many pages did he read on Sunday?

_____ He read _____ pages on Sunday.

8. The Garcias ate 9 pieces of toast for breakfast. If there are 33 slices of bread left, how many slices were in the loaf of bread?

_____ There were _____ slices in the loaf of bread.

9. In a 25-kilometer triathlon, competitors swim 2 kilometers, run 5 kilometers, and bike the rest. How far do they bike?

_____ They bike _____ kilometers.

Lesson 12.6 Solving Multiplication and Division Equations

Division Property of Equality: When two expressions are equal, if they are divided by the same number, the quotients will also be equal.

$a = b$
$a \div c = b \div c$
$\frac{a}{c} = \frac{b}{c}$

Multiplication Property of Equality: When two expressions are equal, if they are multiplied by the same number, the products will also be equal.

$a = b$
$a \times c = b \times c$

Use these properties to solve equations.

$3 \times n = 15$
$\frac{3 \times n}{3} = \frac{15}{3}$
$n = 5$

$n \div 6 = 8$
$n \div 6 \times 6 = 8 \times 6$
$n = 48$

Solve each equation.

a	b	c
1. $2 \times d = 18$ _____	$a \times 4 = 20$ _____	$5 \times n = 30$ _____
2. $y \div 3 = 4$ _____	$t \div 9 = 3$ _____	$\frac{a}{5} = 3$ _____
3. $8 \times s = 64$ _____	$p \times 16 = 16$ _____	$7 \times r = 42$ _____
4. $\frac{n}{5} = 10$ _____	$n \div 3 = 12$ _____	$a \div 8 = 6$ _____
5. $25 = 5 \times d$ _____	$0 = a \times 57$ _____	$32 = b \times 2$ _____
6. $19 = \frac{x}{1}$ _____	$7 = b \div 4$ _____	$9 = \frac{c}{7}$ _____

Write an equation for each problem. Then, solve the equation.

7. Taryn practiced piano the same amount of time every day for 6 days. If she practiced a total of 12 hours, how many hours did she practice each day?

_____ She practiced _____ hours each day.

8. A group of friends decided to equally share a package of trading cards. If there were 48 cards in the package and each person received 12, how many friends were in the group?

_____ There were _____ friends in the group.

9. Twenty-five cars can take the ferry across the river at one time. If 150 cars took the ferry, and it was full each time, how many times did the ferry cross the river?

_____ The ferry crossed the river _____ times.

Lesson 12.7   Adding and Subtracting Integers

The sum of two positive integers is positive.

$$4 + 3 = 7$$

The sum of two negative integers is negative.

$$-4 + (-3) = -7$$

To find the sum of two integers with different signs, find their absolute values. **Absolute value** is the distance (in units) that a number is from 0 expressed as a positive quantity. Subtract the lesser number from the greater number. Absolute value is written as $|X|$.

$$-4 + 3 = -1$$
$$|-4| = 4 \quad 4 - 3 = 1$$

$4 > 3$, so the sum is negative.

The sum has the same sign as the integer with the larger absolute value.

To subtract an integer, add its opposite.

$$5 - 7 = 5 + (-7) = -2$$

Add or subtract.

	a	b	c	d
1.	$6 + 2 =$ _____	$9 + (-4) =$ _____	$7 + (-9) =$ _____	$-3 + 8 =$ _____
2.	$3 - 11 =$ _____	$5 - 2 =$ _____	$-4 - 6 =$ _____	$8 - (-2) =$ _____
3.	$-4 + 7 =$ _____	$-3 + (-6) =$ _____	$-12 + 11 =$ _____	$-16 + (-7) =$ _____
4.	$-12 - 3 =$ _____	$-5 - (-6) =$ _____	$14 - 19 =$ _____	$7 - 18 =$ _____
5.	$-16 + 0 =$ _____	$13 + (-24) =$ _____	$-6 + 8 =$ _____	$-3 + (-2) =$ _____
6.	$4 - 19 =$ _____	$-11 - (-1) =$ _____	$16 - (-27) =$ _____	$7 - 22 =$ _____
7.	$0 + (-9) =$ _____	$-1 + 2 =$ _____	$1 + (-2) =$ _____	$8 + (-8) =$ _____
8.	$-6 - (-6) =$ _____	$-11 - 0 =$ _____	$-2 - 2 =$ _____	$1 - 2 =$ _____
9.	$-4 + 4 =$ _____	$3 + (-6) =$ _____	$7 + (-17) =$ _____	$6 + 5 =$ _____
10.	$8 - 1 =$ _____	$8 - (-1) =$ _____	$-13 - 3 =$ _____	$-4 - (-8) =$ _____

Lesson 12.8 Multiplying and Dividing Integers

The product of two integers with the same sign is positive.

$3 \times 3 = 9$
$-3 \times -3 = 9$

The product of two integers with different signs is negative.

$3 \times (-3) = -9$
$-3 \times 3 = -9$

The quotient of two integers with the same sign is positive.

$8 \div 2 = 4$
$-8 \div (-2) = 4$

The quotient of two integers with different signs is negative.

$8 \div (-2) = -4$
$-8 \div 2 = -4$

Multiply or divide.

	a	b	c	d
1.	$3 \times 2 =$	$-4 \times 6 =$	$8 \times (-3) =$	$-3 \times (-4) =$
2.	$12 \div 4 =$	$16 \div (-4) =$	$-8 \div 4 =$	$9 \div (-3) =$
3.	$-8 \times 7 =$	$6 \times (-5) =$	$-3 \times (-8) =$	$-4 \times 11 =$
4.	$7 \div (-1) =$	$-14 \div 7 =$	$24 \div (-6) =$	$28 \div 7 =$
5.	$16 \times (-2) =$	$-4 \times (-1) =$	$8 \times (-11) =$	$-7 \times (-10) =$
6.	$81 \div (-3) =$	$-63 \div 9 =$	$-55 \div (-5) =$	$18 \div 9 =$
7.	$5 \times 8 =$	$6 \times (-6) =$	$-13 \times (-2) =$	$-9 \times 9 =$
8.	$21 \div (-7) =$	$-38 \div 2 =$	$-19 \div (-1) =$	$-56 \div 8 =$
9.	$17 \times (-1) =$	$5 \times (-2) =$	$-14 \times 3 =$	$-7 \times (-5) =$
10.	$12 \div (-12) =$	$42 \div (-21) =$	$-60 \div (-10) =$	$54 \div (-6) =$

Lesson 12.9 Multiplying and Dividing Powers

A **power** is a number that is expressed using an **exponent**. The **base** is the number that is multiplied, and the exponent tells how many times the base is used as a factor.

base

exponent

$$2^3 = 2 \times 2 \times 2 = 8$$

To multiply powers with the same base, combine bases, add the exponents, then simplify.

$$2^2 \times 2^3 = 2^{2+3} = 2^5 = 32$$

To divide powers with the same base, combine bases, subtract the exponents, then simplify.

$$3^5 \div 3^2 = 3^{5-2} = 3^3 = 27$$

Find the value of each expression.

	a	b	c
1.	$7^2 = $ _____	$8^3 = $ _____	$4^3 = $ _____
2.	$10^2 = $ _____	$9^4 = $ _____	$11^5 = $ _____
3.	$17^3 = $ _____	$5^6 = $ _____	$6^4 = $ _____
4.	$21^3 = $ _____	$16^4 = $ _____	$12^5 = $ _____

Rewrite each expression as one base and one exponent. Then, find the value.

5. $8^2 \times 8^3 = $ _8^5; 32768_ $3^3 \times 3^3 = $ _____ $2^2 \times 2^2 = $ _____

6. $7^4 \div 7^2 = $ _____ $9^5 \div 9^3 = $ _____ $16^4 \div 16^2 = $ _____

7. $6^4 \times 6^1 = $ _____ $4^4 \times 4^2 = $ _____ $3^2 \times 3^2 = $ _____

8. $10^6 \div 10^4 = $ _____ $8^3 \div 8^2 = $ _____ $7^6 \div 7^3 = $ _____

9. $5^3 \times 5^2 = $ _____ $10^3 \times 10^4 = $ _____ $15^2 \times 15^1 = $ _____

10. $2^8 \div 2^3 = $ _____ $3^9 \div 3^7 = $ _____ $6^6 \div 6^3 = $ _____

Lesson 12.10 Negative Exponents

When a power includes a negative exponent, express the number as 1 divided by the base and change the exponent to positive.

$$4^{-2} = \frac{1}{4^2}$$
$$= \frac{1}{16}$$
$$= 0.0625$$

To multiply or divide powers with the same base, combine bases, add or subtract the exponents, then simplify.

$$2^{-3} \times 2^{-2} = 2^{-5} = \frac{1}{2^5} = 0.03125$$
$$2^{-4} \div 2^{-2} = 2^{-2} = \frac{1}{2^2} = 0.25$$

Rewrite each expression with a positive exponent. Then, solve.
Round your answer to four decimal places.

	a	b	c
1.	$3^{-2} =$ _____	$6^{-3} =$ _____	$8^{-2} =$ _____
2.	$7^{-3} =$ _____	$3^{-3} =$ _____	$9^{-2} =$ _____
3.	$4^{-3} =$ _____	$5^{-2} =$ _____	$2^{-3} =$ _____
4.	$2^{-4} =$ _____	$10^{-3} =$ _____	$1^{-4} =$ _____

Find each product. Round your answer to five decimal places.

5.	$4^{-2} \times 4^{-3} =$ _____	$2^{-4} \times 2^{-1} =$ _____	$3^{-2} \times 3^{-3} =$ _____
6.	$6^{-2} \times 6^{-2} =$ _____	$5^{-2} \times 5^{-4} =$ _____	$3^{-2} \times 3^{-2} =$ _____
7.	$8^{-6} \times 8^{4} =$ _____	$7^{-5} \times 7^{2} =$ _____	$2^{-7} \times 2^{4} =$ _____

Find each quotient. Round your answer to five decimal places.

8.	$4^{-4} \div 4^{-2} =$ _____	$8^{-5} \div 8^{-3} =$ _____	$3^{-5} \div 3^{-2} =$ _____
9.	$2^{-8} \div 2^{-4} =$ _____	$5^{-6} \div 5^{-4} =$ _____	$6^{-7} \div 6^{-4} =$ _____
10.	$3^{-3} \div 3^{2} =$ _____	$4^{-3} \div 4^{1} =$ _____	$2^{-6} \div 2^{-3} =$ _____

Check What You Learned

Preparing for Algebra

Write each phrase as a numerical expression.

	a	**b**
1.	seven less than a number	eight more than a number
2.	the product of six and a number	a number divided by twelve

Write each sentence as an equation.

3. The product of four and a number is sixteen.   Nine more than n is 11.

4. Three less than a number is twenty.   Twenty-five divided by b is five.

Solve each equation.

	a	**b**	**c**
5.	$5 + n = 12$	$n + 3 = 8$	$4 + d = 25$
6.	$18 = n + 6$	$27 = 9 + b$	$32 = 20 + c$
7.	$5 - n = 0$	$15 - b = 7$	$23 - a = 12$
8.	$9 = 10 - d$	$26 = 30 - n$	$7 = 42 \div s$
9.	$2 \times b = 18$	$7 \times f = 35$	$r \times 6 = 30$
10.	$45 = n \times 9$	$62 = 2 \times b$	$66 = 11 \times t$
11.	$n \div 3 = 11$	$b \div 6 = 9$	$a \div 2 = 8$
12.	$14 = b \div 2$	$7 = c \div 3$	$3 = n \div 8$

Check What You Learned

Preparing for Algebra

Find the value of each expression. Round to five decimal places if necessary.

	a	b	c
13.	$30 \div (6 - 1) =$ _____	$(3 + 2) \times 3 =$ _____	$(6 - 2) \times 4 =$ _____
14.	$3 + 15 \div 3 =$ _____	$(3 + 15) \div 3 =$ _____	$10 - 4 \times 2 =$ _____
15.	$-6 + 4 =$ _____	$7 + (-3) =$ _____	$-5 + (-2) =$ _____
16.	$-9 + 12 =$ _____	$8 + (-11) =$ _____	$-4 + (-8) =$ _____
17.	$13 - 16 =$ _____	$9 - (-8) =$ _____	$-3 - 7 =$ _____
18.	$-7 - (-4) =$ _____	$12 - (-3) =$ _____	$-9 - 1 =$ _____
19.	$-3 \times 4 =$ _____	$6 \times (-3) =$ _____	$-2 \times (-8) =$ _____
20.	$-5 \times (-6) =$ _____	$7 \times (-9) =$ _____	$-6 \times (-1) =$ _____
21.	$-18 \div 9 =$ _____	$24 \div (-6) =$ _____	$-40 \div (-4) =$ _____
22.	$-6 \div 6 =$ _____	$17 \div (-1) =$ _____	$-46 \div 2 =$ _____
23.	$2^2 \times 2^2 =$ _____	$3^3 \times 3^2 =$ _____	$6^2 \times 6^1 =$ _____
24.	$7^5 \div 7^3 =$ _____	$8^6 \div 8^3 =$ _____	$5^5 \div 5^2 =$ _____
25.	$3^{-2} \times 3^{-1} =$ _____	$2^{-3} \times 2^{-2} =$ _____	$4^{-3} \times 4^1 =$ _____
26.	$3^{-2} \div 3^{-1} =$ _____	$7^{-6} \div 7^{-3} =$ _____	$2^2 \div 2^4 =$ _____

Final Test Chapters 1–12

Multiply or divide. Write answers in simplest form.

	a	b	c	d
1.	$\frac{1}{8} \times \frac{3}{5}$ _____	$\frac{2}{3} \times \frac{3}{7}$ _____	$3\frac{1}{7} \times \frac{5}{8}$ _____	$2\frac{1}{3} \times 1\frac{3}{8}$ _____
2.	$\frac{3}{8} \times 1\frac{5}{6}$ _____	$2\frac{1}{7} \times 1\frac{1}{3}$ _____	$6\frac{1}{2} \times 2\frac{1}{3}$ _____	$3\frac{5}{8} \times \frac{2}{9}$ _____
3.	$\frac{6}{7} \div \frac{1}{2}$ _____	$\frac{3}{5} \div \frac{7}{10}$ _____	$\frac{5}{8} \div \frac{1}{3}$ _____	$1\frac{2}{3} \div \frac{3}{5}$ _____
4.	$3\frac{4}{5} \div 1\frac{1}{2}$ _____	$4\frac{1}{4} \div 3\frac{3}{8}$ _____	$6\frac{1}{2} \div \frac{1}{5}$ _____	$2\frac{1}{3} \div 2$ _____

Complete the following table.

	Principal	Rate	Time	Interest	Total Amount
5.	$350	4%	$1\frac{1}{2}$ years	_____	_____
6.	$720	$5\frac{1}{4}$%	3 years	_____	_____
7.	$1340	$8\frac{1}{2}$%	$\frac{1}{2}$ year	_____	_____
8.	$600	3%	$4\frac{3}{4}$ years	_____	_____

Solve each of the following.

	a	b	c
9.	$\frac{3}{5} = \frac{n}{20}$ _____	$\frac{n}{6} = \frac{12}{18}$ _____	$\frac{4}{n} = \frac{10}{20}$ _____
10.	$\frac{5}{8} = \frac{15}{n}$ _____	$\frac{8}{25} = \frac{n}{100}$ _____	$\frac{12}{n} = \frac{1}{3}$ _____

Spectrum Math
Grade 7

Final Test
Chapters 1–12
165

CHAPTERS 1–12 FINAL TEST

Final Test   Chapters 1–12

Convert the following.

	a	b	c
11.	$3\frac{1}{4}$ mi. = _____ yd.	5 ft. 3 in. = _____ in.	3.5 lb. = _____ oz.
12.	78 hr. = _____ days	223 min. = __ hr. __ min.	$1\frac{3}{4}$ gal. = _____ pt.
13.	340 m = _____ km	0.7 m = _____ cm	1.2 g = _____ mg
14.	350 L = _____ kL	1246 g = _____ kg	1382 mL = _____ L

Use this data set to complete the following.

Score on quiz: 9, 18, 12, 9, 13, 22, 8, 23, 16, 17, 22, 20, 22, 15, 10, 17, 21, 23, 14, 11

15. Make a stem-and-leaf plot.

16. Draw in the bars to complete the histogram.

Quiz Scores

17. Find the mean, median, mode, and range of the data.

mean: _____   mode: _____

median: _____   range: _____

18. What percent of the people scored 16–20 points?   _____%

19. What was the highest quiz score?   _____

20. What was the lowest quiz score?   _____

21. What percent of the scores are 21–25 points?   _____%

Spectrum Math
Grade 7
166

Final Test
Chapters 1–12

CHAPTERS 1–12 FINAL TEST

Final Test Chapters 1–12

Find the perimeter of each figure.

	a	**b**	**c**

22.

7 yd. 3 yd.
3 yd. 7 yd.

_____ yd.

2 m
1.5 m
3 m 2 m

_____ m

7 in. 9 in.
12 in.

_____ in.

Find the area of each figure.

23.

14 cm
18 cm

_____ sq. cm

18 mm

_____ sq. mm

8 ft.
22 ft.

_____ sq. ft.

Find the circumference and area of each circle. Use 3.14 for pi.

24.

8 cm

12 in.

18 yd.

circumference: _____ cm   _____ in.   _____ yd.

area: _____ sq. cm   _____ sq. in.   _____ sq. yd.

Find the surface area of each figure. Use 3.14 for pi.

25.

12 in.
10 in.
13 in.

_____ sq. in.

42 ft.
8 ft.

_____ sq. ft.

7.5 cm
2 cm
8 cm

_____ sq. cm

Spectrum Math
Grade 7

Final Test
Chapters 1–12

CHAPTERS 1–12 FINAL TEST

167

Final Test   Chapters 1–12

Find the volume of each figure. Use 3.14 for pi.

26.

3 in.
12 in.

6 cm
11 cm   9.5 cm

2.5 m   8 m
3 m

_____ cubic in.   _____ cubic cm   _____ cubic m

Solve each equation.

	a	**b**	**c**
27.	$6 + c = 23$ _____	$d + 11 = 15$ _____	$28 = a + 9$ _____
28.	$32 - r = 15$ _____	$p - 13 = 5$ _____	$7 = 15 - n$ _____
29.	$8 \times b = 48$ _____	$7 \times d = 21$ _____	$33 = 3 \times t$ _____
30.	$a \div 5 = 5$ _____	$n \div 8 = 5$ _____	$6 = m \div 10$ _____

Find the value of each expression. Round to five decimal places if necessary.

31. $(3 + 2) \times 10 =$ _____ $24 \div (8 - 4) =$ _____ $6 + 4 \times 7 =$ _____

32. $-4 + 2 =$ _____ $3 + (-8) =$ _____ $2 + (-3) =$ _____

33. $-10 - 4 =$ _____ $-9 - (-6) =$ _____ $15 - (-11) =$ _____

34. $6 \times (-2) =$ _____ $-4 \times 3 =$ _____ $-3 \times (-9) =$ _____

35. $-8 \div 4 =$ _____ $12 \div (-6) =$ _____ $-14 \div (-2) =$ _____

36. $2 + 3 \times (-4) =$ _____ $(-3 + 2) \times 5 =$ _____ $-4 \times 5 \div 2 =$ _____

37. $2^2 \times 2^1 =$ _____ $3^2 \times 3^2 =$ _____ $2^3 \times 2^2 =$ _____

38. $2^{-2} \div 2^3 =$ _____ $3^{-3} \div 3^{-2} =$ _____ $2^{-6} \div 2^{-4} =$ _____

39. $20 \div (-5) + 3 =$ _____ $2 + (-3) + 1 =$ _____ $-3 \times 4 + 6 =$ _____

40. $3^2 + 4 =$ _____ $2^3 - 4 =$ _____ $4^2 - 9 =$ _____

CHAPTERS 1–12 FINAL TEST

Spectrum Math
Grade 7
168

Final Test
Chapters 1–12

Scoring Record for Posttests, Mid-Test, and Final Test

Chapter Posttest	Your Score	Performance			
		Excellent	Very Good	Fair	Needs Improvement
1	____ of 36	34–36	30–33	23–29	22 or fewer
2	____ of 26	25–26	22–24	17–21	16 or fewer
3	____ of 30	29–30	25–28	19–24	18 or fewer
4	____ of 39	37–39	32–36	24–31	23 or fewer
5	____ of 40	38–40	33–37	25–32	24 or fewer
6	____ of 22	21–22	19–20	14–18	13 or fewer
7	____ of 68	57–60	49–56	37–48	36 or fewer
8	____ of 37	34–36	30–33	23–29	22 or fewer
9	____ of 20	20	17–19	13–16	12 or fewer
10	____ of 40	38–40	33–37	25–32	24 or fewer
11	____ of 38	36–38	31–35	24–30	23 or fewer
12	____ of 74	70–74	60–69	45–59	44 or fewer
Mid-Test	____ of 83	78–83	67–77	51–66	50 or fewer
Final Test	____ of 113	106–113	91–105	69–90	68 or fewer

Record your test score in the Your Score column. See where your score falls in the Performance columns. Your score is based on the total number of required responses. If your score is fair or needs improvement, review the chapter material.

Grade 7 Answers

Chapter 1

Pretest, page 1

	a	b	c	d	e
1.	145	999	8775	149795	1002996
2.	66	278	841	37368	165267
3.	476	26961	34758	42258	252711
4.	1591	135432	525586	1346235	979232
5.	7	247r2	761r2	12r2	21r8
6.	13r11	322	226r35	288r11	1413r2

Pretest, page 2

7. 138 **8.** 37 **9.** $1764 **10.** 587529

11. $117480 **12.** 154; 18

Lesson 1.1, page 3

	a	b	c	d	e
1.	392	178	943	15519	757609
2.	127	747	8056	79807	320840
3.	981	1240	4792	96064	869998
4.	178	898	8911	47693	819274
5.	119	980	7928	78850	776414

Lesson 1.2, page 4

	a	b	c	d	e
1.	31	594	4109	21116	82327
2.	16	187	6787	22296	582109
3.	85	294	3084	37611	791087
4.	8	291	4917	88912	44089
5.	59	149	916	57082	239981
6.	23	263	2691	58091	317818

Lesson 1.3, page 5

1. $3 **2.** 82206 **3.** 11729 **4.** $1050 **5.** 9430

6. 359 **7.** 1098

Lesson 1.4, page 6

	a	b	c	d
1.	148	4774	1578	10865
2.	2438	18424	27072	414143
3.	1972	121401	195415	1718412
4.	17316	196176	1146140	585044

Lesson 1.5, page 7

	a	b	c	d	e
1.	6r1	29	53r3	68	778
2.	9r2	37r1	85r2	543r3	172r5
3.	14	17r4	175r1	2064r1	1930r3

Lesson 1.6, page 8

	a	b	c	d	e
1.	34r1	27r20	3r30	7r14	11r48
2.	26r22	6r42	38r6	3r16	7
3.	18r28	23	6r5	33r13	26r29

Lesson 1.6, page 9

	a	b	c	d	e
1.	273r5	94r71	606	1259r47	635r56
2.	176r17	237	211r25	2281r18	6428r3
3.	249	107r53	376r42	1014r59	447

Lesson 1.7, page 10

1. 6; 39 **2.** 9450 **3.** 427 **4.** 118990 **5.** 47

6. 670560 **7.** 6; 16

Posttest, page 11

	a	b	c	d	e
1.	173	1573	14048	212666	1172870
2.	84	443	1604	15991	377917
3.	2992	70176	7968	17232	37944
4.	7553	360240	282576	708876	1288686
5.	12r1	222r3	1917r1	24r8	13r5
6.	94r5	278r16	111r21	406r85	351

Posttest, page 12

7. 1626 **8.** 792 **9.** 11; 17 **10.** 1635

11. 3650 **12.** 2851

Chapter 2

Pretest, page 13

	a	b	c	d
1.	$4\frac{11}{12}$	$5\frac{9}{14}$	$6\frac{19}{24}$	$4\frac{18}{35}$
2.	$4\frac{1}{12}$	$\frac{1}{8}$	$2\frac{1}{2}$	$2\frac{1}{14}$
3.	$\frac{1}{8}$	$\frac{10}{21}$	$\frac{2}{9}$	$\frac{21}{320}$
4.	$3\frac{5}{24}$	$6\frac{7}{8}$	$6\frac{2}{7}$	$2\frac{1}{6}$
5.	$3\frac{9}{11}$	$\frac{23}{42}$	$2\frac{1}{2}$	$\frac{16}{19}$

Pretest, page 14

6. $10\frac{1}{24}$ **7.** $26\frac{1}{6}$ **8.** $6\frac{1}{4}$ **9.** $6\frac{1}{2}$ **10.** $21\frac{2}{3}$ **11.** $9\frac{7}{24}$

Lesson 2.1, page 15

1. 1, 2, 7, 14
   1, 3, 7, 21; 1, 7; 7
2. 1, 2, 3, 4, 6, 12
   1, 2, 4, 5, 10, 20; 1, 2, 4; 4
3. 1, 2, 5, 10
   1, 2, 3, 4, 6, 12; 1, 2; 2
4. 1, 2, 3, 4, 6, 8, 12, 24
   1, 2, 3, 4, 6, 9, 12, 18, 36; 1, 2, 3, 4, 6, 12; 12
5. 1, 3, 9
   1, 3, 5, 15; 1, 3; 3
6. 1, 2, 3, 6
   1, 2, 4, 8; 1, 2; 2
7. 1, 2, 3, 6, 9, 18
   1, 2, 4, 5, 10, 20; 1, 2; 2

Grade 7 Answers

Lesson 2.2, page 16

	a	b	c
1.	$\frac{9}{10}$	$3\frac{3}{4}$	$\frac{5}{19}$
2.	$\frac{1}{2}$	$\frac{9}{10}$	$9\frac{2}{3}$
3.	$\frac{3}{4}$	$7\frac{1}{3}$	$\frac{3}{4}$
4.	$8\frac{3}{4}$	$6\frac{1}{4}$	$4\frac{5}{7}$
5.	$4\frac{1}{5}$	$\frac{1}{2}$	$2\frac{3}{13}$

Lesson 2.3, page 17

	a	b
1.	$\frac{5}{30}$ and $\frac{12}{30}$	$\frac{9}{24}$ and $\frac{8}{24}$
2.	$\frac{21}{28}$ and $\frac{4}{28}$	$\frac{2}{12}$ and $\frac{9}{12}$
3.	$\frac{4}{8}$ and $\frac{5}{8}$	$\frac{5}{20}$ and $\frac{6}{20}$
4.	$\frac{9}{45}$ and $\frac{20}{45}$	$\frac{8}{20}$ and $\frac{5}{20}$
5.	$\frac{5}{15}$ and $\frac{9}{15}$	$\frac{3}{18}$ and $\frac{4}{18}$

Lesson 2.4, page 18

	a	b	c	d
1.	$\frac{29}{8}$	$\frac{9}{1}$	$\frac{17}{7}$	$\frac{11}{2}$
2.	$\frac{9}{8}$	$\frac{33}{4}$	$\frac{14}{1}$	$\frac{23}{6}$
3.	$\frac{13}{3}$	$\frac{43}{9}$	$\frac{7}{5}$	$\frac{47}{1}$
4.	$3\frac{1}{3}$	$2\frac{7}{8}$	$1\frac{1}{2}$	$5\frac{4}{7}$
5.	$3\frac{3}{4}$	$5\frac{2}{3}$	$1\frac{1}{2}$	$6\frac{2}{3}$
6.	$1\frac{8}{11}$	$4\frac{1}{5}$	$9\frac{2}{5}$	$4\frac{8}{11}$

Lesson 2.5, page 19

	a	b	c	d
1.	$1\frac{3}{8}$	$\frac{5}{6}$	$1\frac{3}{20}$	$\frac{1}{2}$
2.	$1\frac{7}{40}$	$\frac{4}{5}$	$\frac{11}{12}$	$1\frac{9}{20}$
3.	$\frac{5}{8}$	$\frac{29}{35}$	$1\frac{1}{56}$	$\frac{13}{15}$
4.	$\frac{7}{20}$	$\frac{1}{5}$	$\frac{3}{8}$	$\frac{7}{15}$
5.	$\frac{1}{2}$	$\frac{7}{15}$	$\frac{11}{24}$	$\frac{1}{5}$
6.	$\frac{1}{12}$	$\frac{1}{18}$	$\frac{1}{6}$	$\frac{41}{99}$

Lesson 2.6, page 20

	a	b	c	d
1.	$3\frac{7}{12}$	$10\frac{7}{8}$	$6\frac{13}{21}$	$4\frac{7}{10}$
2.	$7\frac{7}{9}$	$2\frac{33}{40}$	$5\frac{19}{24}$	$3\frac{22}{35}$
3.	$5\frac{3}{4}$	$4\frac{7}{18}$	$4\frac{47}{70}$	$6\frac{5}{6}$
4.	$1\frac{11}{72}$	$1\frac{11}{12}$	$\frac{3}{4}$	$1\frac{43}{56}$
5.	$1\frac{49}{88}$	$4\frac{4}{5}$	$2\frac{5}{6}$	$1\frac{23}{42}$
6.	$2\frac{1}{9}$	$1\frac{9}{20}$	$2\frac{17}{24}$	$1\frac{3}{8}$

Lesson 2.7, page 21

1. $\frac{3}{4}$ 2. $13\frac{31}{40}$ 3. $9\frac{7}{12}$ 4. $\frac{3}{4}$ 5. $3\frac{31}{56}$; $1\frac{17}{56}$ 6. $2\frac{11}{24}$

Lesson 2.8, page 22

	a	b	c	d
1.	$\frac{3}{8}$	$\frac{8}{15}$	$\frac{9}{16}$	$\frac{1}{10}$
2.	$\frac{21}{40}$	$\frac{1}{5}$	$\frac{3}{35}$	$\frac{6}{25}$
3.	$\frac{15}{64}$	$\frac{1}{3}$	$\frac{5}{9}$	$\frac{4}{21}$
4.	$\frac{1}{9}$	$\frac{1}{5}$	$\frac{16}{105}$	$\frac{5}{48}$
5.	$\frac{3}{32}$	$\frac{1}{8}$	$\frac{3}{14}$	$\frac{1}{12}$
6.	$\frac{3}{35}$	$\frac{1}{30}$	$\frac{7}{60}$	$\frac{3}{8}$

Lesson 2.9, page 23

	a	b	c
1.	$3\frac{6}{7}$	$7\frac{1}{2}$	$3\frac{11}{18}$
2.	$13\frac{1}{2}$	$6\frac{11}{24}$	$2\frac{6}{7}$
3.	$31\frac{1}{2}$	$17\frac{1}{2}$	$94\frac{7}{8}$
4.	$2\frac{2}{9}$	$3\frac{25}{48}$	$4\frac{1}{2}$
5.	$1\frac{11}{16}$	$3\frac{1}{18}$	$3\frac{2}{3}$
6.	$12\frac{4}{7}$	$1\frac{2}{3}$	$\frac{35}{36}$

Lesson 2.10, page 24

	a	b	c	d	e	f
1.	$\frac{3}{2}$	$\frac{8}{9}$	$\frac{2}{7}$	$\frac{4}{13}$	$\frac{12}{9}$	$\frac{5}{2}$
2.	$\frac{8}{7}$	$\frac{3}{10}$	$\frac{5}{8}$	$\frac{1}{12}$	$\frac{7}{3}$	2
3.	10	$\frac{5}{3}$	$\frac{7}{15}$	$\frac{11}{3}$	$\frac{8}{19}$	$\frac{1}{4}$
4.	$\frac{8}{3}$	$\frac{7}{2}$	$\frac{9}{4}$	$\frac{4}{7}$	$\frac{12}{7}$	$\frac{14}{3}$
5.	$\frac{17}{2}$	15	$\frac{20}{13}$	$\frac{9}{20}$	$\frac{1}{3}$	$\frac{7}{25}$
6.	$\frac{1}{5}$	$\frac{2}{5}$	$\frac{5}{3}$	$\frac{12}{13}$	$\frac{11}{14}$	$\frac{16}{3}$
7.	$\frac{7}{17}$	$\frac{1}{20}$	$\frac{9}{8}$	$\frac{16}{53}$	$\frac{8}{17}$	16

Lesson 2.11, page 25

	a	b	c	d
1.	$5\frac{1}{4}$	$2\frac{8}{15}$	$1\frac{1}{2}$	$21\frac{1}{3}$
2.	$11\frac{2}{3}$	$1\frac{9}{16}$	$2\frac{6}{7}$	$\frac{3}{5}$
3.	$11\frac{1}{4}$	$\frac{3}{5}$	$3\frac{1}{3}$	$2\frac{1}{6}$
4.	10	$10\frac{15}{16}$	51	98
5.	$2\frac{1}{45}$	$1\frac{47}{63}$	$\frac{4}{5}$	$\frac{14}{15}$

Lesson 2.11, page 26

	a	b	c	d
1.	$2\frac{1}{2}$	$1\frac{81}{119}$	$1\frac{15}{26}$	$1\frac{3}{4}$
2.	$\frac{8}{17}$	$9\frac{3}{4}$	6	$\frac{14}{15}$
3.	$2\frac{2}{11}$	$1\frac{11}{12}$	$1\frac{19}{22}$	30

Grade 7 Answers

4. $1\frac{20}{33}$ 28 $\frac{9}{10}$ $5\frac{5}{7}$

5. $6\frac{1}{14}$ $\frac{17}{22}$ $1\frac{11}{16}$ $2\frac{5}{14}$

6. $\frac{7}{24}$ 30 $2\frac{14}{15}$ $3\frac{13}{15}$

Lesson 2.12, page 27

	a	b	c	d
1.	$\frac{1}{8}$	$\frac{14}{39}$	$\frac{12}{35}$	$\frac{1}{8}$
2.	$\frac{5}{24}$	$\frac{10}{27}$	$\frac{5}{168}$	$\frac{1}{5}$
3.	$\frac{7}{10}$	$1\frac{29}{56}$	$1\frac{1}{8}$	$4\frac{41}{96}$
4.	$\frac{5}{6}$	$3\frac{19}{24}$	$12\frac{6}{7}$	$11\frac{47}{56}$
5.	$2\frac{1}{10}$	$1\frac{1}{2}$	$1\frac{1}{24}$	$8\frac{1}{3}$
6.	4	$5\frac{1}{4}$	$\frac{104}{119}$	$1\frac{5}{8}$
7.	$1\frac{29}{45}$	$1\frac{43}{78}$	$\frac{1}{5}$	$2\frac{4}{27}$

Lesson 2.13, page 28

1. $\frac{2}{3}$ **2.** $14\frac{7}{12}$ **3.** 5 **4.** $\frac{1}{4}$ **5.** $3\frac{1}{3}$ **6.** $14\frac{5}{8}$

7. $74\frac{2}{3}$

Posttest, page 29

	a	b	c	d
1.	$2\frac{5}{56}$	$5\frac{7}{12}$	$4\frac{17}{24}$	$7\frac{1}{8}$
2.	$3\frac{5}{12}$	$\frac{3}{8}$	$2\frac{31}{70}$	$2\frac{5}{12}$
3.	$\frac{3}{10}$	$\frac{3}{14}$	$\frac{5}{27}$	$\frac{1}{48}$
4.	$2\frac{3}{56}$	$3\frac{15}{28}$	$6\frac{13}{18}$	$10\frac{1}{2}$
5.	$2\frac{55}{144}$	$\frac{11}{24}$	$3\frac{13}{14}$	6

Posttest, page 30

6. $2\frac{1}{24}$ **7.** $3\frac{1}{4}$ **8.** $6; \frac{3}{7}$ **9.** $1\frac{1}{2}$ **10.** $5\frac{7}{12}$ **11.** $13\frac{3}{4}$

Chapter 3

Pretest, page 31

	a	b	c	d
1.	8.94	27.763	9.244	9.1360
2.	2.8	13.103	12.764	3.9133
3.	6.24	7.038	2.52604	8.74698
4.	0.52	.305	.834	3.4187
5.	4	2400	38.6	12000
6.	4.2	3.11	8.6	14.4

Pretest, page 32

7. 2.45 **8.** 353.8 **9.** $3.02 **10.** $12.38

11. 91.75 **12.** 183.875

Lesson 3.1, page 33

	a	b	c
1.	1.6	2.25	0.240
2.	2.5	5.24	2.046
3.	5.8	1.35	6.628
4.	6.2	2.90	3.720
5.	3.7420	4.1120	1.5148
6.	$\frac{3}{10}$	$1\frac{3}{5}$	$3\frac{7}{10}$
7.	$\frac{3}{4}$	$5\frac{43}{50}$	$1\frac{13}{100}$
8.	$\frac{387}{1000}$	$2\frac{147}{250}$	$3\frac{9}{100}$
9.	$\frac{5329}{10000}$	$6\frac{4273}{10000}$	$5\frac{233}{400}$

Lesson 3.2, page 34

	a	b	c	d	e
1.	1.1	4.0	4.3	7.7	13.3
2.	0.91	3.45	3.57	7.62	1.94
3.	0.499	4.327	6.237	5.513	9.717
4.	4.245	2.314	22.427	3.8600	7.8239
5.	5.7047	14.0272	65.437	3.281	7.3883
6.	4.938	3.8366	6.3361	7.417	4.6694

Lesson 3.3, page 35

	a	b	c	d	e
1.	0.5	0.88	0.94	2.181	2.881
2.	0.16	0.067	1.68	0.696	0.801
3.	0.114	1.873	20.567	2.069	39.329
4.	8.295	17.513	26.44	6.863	0.281
5.	0.173	2.813	29.22	2.14	2.693
6.	46.407	0.873	2.62	1.029	5.558

Lesson 3.4, page 36

1. 0.347 **2.** $25.12 **3.** $4.02 **4.** 115.84

5. $22.42 **6.** 1.433 **7.** 0.705

Lesson 3.5, page 37

	a	b	c	d	e
1.	3.6	2.44	6.96	3.636	65.4
2.	5.55	17.472	2.8721	2.6334	4.48100
3.	5.566	1.4602	30.102	5.139	4.41234
4.	18.21	2.3304	2.12403	3.48	44.5278

Lesson 3.6, page 38

	a	b	c	d
1.	0.12	3.8	0.35	3.01
2.	0.909	0.411	5.008	0.6774
3.	0.0032	0.77	0.807	0.514
4.	0.116	0.902	0.0211	1.0907

Grade 7 Answers

Lesson 3.7, page 39

	a	b	c	d
1.	140	50	600	100
2.	30	4	400	7000
3.	5	200	1500	2000
4.	120	1600	44000	172000

Lesson 3.8, page 40

	a	b	c	d
1.	1520	12	4.4	3.75
2.	3.9	63	36.5	6.282
3.	31.55	243	6.335	4.225
4.	0.65	21.7	17.5	1.4

Lesson 3.9, page 41

	a	b	c	d
1.	0.26	11.362	1.8855	6.34524
2.	53.94	0.30702	14.0196	0.71706
3.	0.12	0.91	0.09	0.006
4.	2.06	4.009	2.711	0.6015
5.	90	30	90	300
6.	36	1.3	33.8	23.7
7.	60000	3.8	2.55	37

Lesson 3.10, page 42

1. $14.95   2. 14.5   3. 17.5   4. 127.75
5. $64.93   6. 0.806   7. 0.88

Posttest, page 43

	a	b	c	d
1.	1.13	79.41	11.845	57.7984
2.	10.8363	32.2458	2.9	26.29
3.	26.983	5.092	2.414	4.2634
4.	2.48	8.6315	47.0352	4.43597
5.	1.36	1.793	260	475
6.	18.91	6	0.39	13.9

Posttest, page 44

7. $36.65   8. 9   9. 0.238   10. $3.53   11. 8.8
12. 29.16

Chapter 4

Pretest, page 45

	a	b	c
1.	82%	35%	60%
2.	350%	725%	30%
3.	0.2	0.38	1.27
4.	0.125	0.076	0.2225
5.	$\frac{1}{4}$	$\frac{2}{5}$	$3\frac{1}{5}$
6.	1.6	14	2.4
7.	99	0.04	60

	a	b	c
8.	32	200	35
9.	17.5	4	30
10.	25%	80%	200%
11.	15%	2%	20%

Pretest, page 46

12. $4.31   13. $763.50   14. $37.40   15. $108.75
16. $2.34   17. $0.48

Lesson 4.1, page 47

1.	$\frac{7}{100}$	0.07
2.	$\frac{13}{100}$	0.13
3.	$\frac{12}{25}$	0.48
4.	$\frac{71}{100}$	0.71
5.	$\frac{27}{100}$	0.27
6.	$\frac{1}{50}$	0.02
7.	$\frac{3}{20}$	0.15
8.	$\frac{39}{100}$	0.39
9.	$\frac{1}{10}$	0.10
10.	$\frac{31}{50}$	0.62
11.	$\frac{3}{4}$	0.75
12.	$\frac{97}{100}$	0.97
13.	$\frac{53}{100}$	0.53
14.	$\frac{41}{50}$	0.82

Lesson 4.2, page 48

	a	b	c
1.	$13\% < \frac{2}{5}$	$0.35 > \frac{1}{8}$	$\frac{1}{4} = 0.25$
2.	$87\% > 0.79$	$18 > 18\%$	$\frac{1}{2} > 0.42$
3.	$\frac{9}{10} > 9\%$	$40\% < \frac{4}{5}$	$0.72 > \frac{2}{3}$
4.	$0.82 = \frac{41}{50}$	$63\% > \frac{1}{2}$	$14\% > 0.014$
5.	$\frac{1}{3} < 50\%$	$\frac{4}{5} = 80\%$	$0.07 < \frac{1}{10}$
6.	$\frac{250}{100} = 2.5$	$0.25 < \frac{1}{3}$	$318 > 3.18\%$
7.	$50\% < \frac{2}{3}$	$93\% = 0.93$	$22\% < \frac{1}{4}$
8.	$0.67 > \frac{3}{5}$	$\frac{1}{2} > 20\%$	$642\% = 6.42$
9.	$0.08 < 80\%$	$50\% < \frac{3}{4}$	$\frac{1}{2} > 0.050$
10.	$\frac{2}{5} < 2.5$	$70\% = \frac{7}{10}$	$\frac{147}{100} > 14\%$
11.	$\frac{45}{100} < 55\%$	$1238\% = 12.38$	$16\frac{2}{5} > 16.25$
12.	$3.75 = 375\%$	$0.15 < \frac{1}{5}$	$7.5 > \frac{3}{4}$
13.	$\frac{13}{25} > 49\%$	$0.45 > \frac{7}{20}$	$3\% = 0.03$
14.	$25\% > \frac{11}{50}$	$12\frac{1}{5} = 12.2$	$18\% < \frac{1}{4}$

Grade 7 Answers

Lesson 4.3, page 49

	a	b
1.	13%, $\frac{1}{4}$, $\frac{1}{3}$, 0.35	0.02, 0.34, 72%, $\frac{3}{4}$
2.	0.25, $\frac{1}{3}$, $\frac{2}{5}$, 45%	1%, $\frac{1}{10}$, $\frac{11}{100}$, 0.15
3.	$\frac{14}{100}$, $\frac{14}{25}$, 143%, 14.5	0.55, $\frac{3}{5}$, 0.63, 68%
4.	$3\frac{1}{2}$, 320%, 35%, $\frac{3}{100}$	0.5, 0.4, 30%, $\frac{1}{4}$, $\frac{1}{5}$
5.	$\frac{7}{8}$, $\frac{3}{4}$, 0.625, 60%	1.7, 17%, $\frac{1}{7}$, 0.017
6.	4.1, 406%, $\frac{4}{5}$, $\frac{40}{100}$	$5\frac{2}{5}$, $\frac{16}{5}$, 32%, 16%

Lesson 4.4, page 50

	a	b	c	d
1.	$\frac{3}{4}$	28	32	$\frac{49}{50}$
2.	$\frac{14}{25}$	$\frac{12}{25}$	240	930
3.	62	45	$\frac{3}{25}$	$4\frac{1}{4}$
4.	760	$\frac{3}{20}$	225	$\frac{31}{100}$
5.	$\frac{3}{5}$	20	50	$\frac{18}{25}$
6.	375	$1\frac{7}{20}$	$\frac{2}{5}$	56
7.	85	$62\frac{1}{2}$	$\frac{13}{20}$	$\frac{1}{10}$
8.	$\frac{1}{20}$	1016	$\frac{1}{2}$	335

Lesson 4.5, page 51

	a	b	c
1.	0.85	147	0.17
2.	38	0.0832	69
3.	0.27	5	0.021
4.	150	0.15	42.6
5.	0.335	65	0.0925
6.	3.9	0.526	485
7.	0.055	22.5	0.0625
8.	0.5	5.25	70
9.	0.001	10	6320

Lesson 4.5, page 52

	a	b	c
1.	0.2525	0.035	0.027
2.	0.1505	0.632	0.1268
3.	0.0575	0.113	0.4275
4.	0.175	0.224	0.7545
5.	0.096	0.1808	0.5225
6.	0.0338	0.391	0.8348
7.	0.152	0.7916	0.2775
8.	0.3895	0.089	0.9372
9.	0.4866	0.034	0.817
10.	0.505	0.145	0.4575

Lesson 4.6, page 53

	a	b	c
1.	12.5	19.5	19.25
2.	14.6	1.6	5.64
3.	3.5	41.85	1.875
4.	3.12	0.88	82.4
5.	1.24	0.36	3.822
6.	2.94	3.48	33.75
7.	0.15	3.3	50.4
8.	8	118.75	48
9.	0.8	10.355	52.25
10.	47.25	395.5	2.45

Lesson 4.6, page 54

	a	b	c
1.	25	25	50
2.	24	200	150
3.	15	140	30
4.	40	75	80
5.	17.25	20	5
6.	20	10	5
7.	1	7.5	55
8.	12.5	25	62.5
9.	85	5	120
10.	500	12.5	100

Lesson 4.6, page 55

	a	b	c
1.	64	35	125
2.	2.5	332	40
3.	300	15	50
4.	290	200	50
5.	19.3	0.5	100
6.	50	15	25
7.	45	78	95
8.	46	56	100
9.	500	73	2
10.	342	15	20

Lesson 4.7, page 56

1. $2.25   2. $4.84   3. $4.95; $94.95   4. 20%
5. $8000   6. 40%

Posttest, page 57

	a	b	c
1.	40	90	15
2.	42	130	1
3.	0.53	2.5	0.08
4.	0.0775	0.292	0.051
5.	$4\frac{3}{4}$	$\frac{3}{5}$	$1\frac{11}{20}$
6.	2	3.8	72
7.	112	0.3	0.008
8.	400	75	15

Grade 7 Answers

9.	0.5	30	50
10.	13.75	5	8
11.	20	1000	165

Posttest, page 58
  12. $4.19 13. $3.57 14. $2.47 15. 20%
  16. 15.625% 17. $379.50

Chapter 5

Pretest, page 59
  1. $31.50; $556.50
  2. $30.40; $410.40
  3. $85.68; $799.68
  4. $87.50; $1,337.50
  5. $135.00; $635.00
  6. $84.50; $734.50
  7. $90.20; $910.20
  8. $139.50; $439.50
  9. $33.75; $1,033.75
  10. $50.05; $570.05
  11. $1,323.00; $5,523.00
  12. $267.75; $1,967.75
  13. $2.00; $52.00
  14. $131.25; $1,531.25
  15. $4.55; $284.55

Pretest, page 60
  16. $51.00; $531.00
  17. $15,750.00; $35,750.00
  18. $3.15; $123.15
  19. $8.25; $58.25
  20. $86.80; $706.80

Lesson 5.1, page 61
  1. $19.50 2. $14.00 3. $16.00
  4. $8.75 5. $17.50 6. $19.50
  7. $16.60 8. $15.94 9. $21.75
  10. $59.50 11. $46.00 12. $46.25
  13. $21.82 14. $96.60

Lesson 5.1, page 62
  1. $45.00 2. $26.00 3. $2.08 4. $105.00
  5. $9.00 6. $33.10 7. $325.00

Lesson 5.2, page 63
  1. $105.00; $605.00
  2. $180.00; $930.00
  3. $161.50; $586.50
  4. $153.00; $753.00
  5. $168.00; $518.00
  6. $73.50; $773.50
  7. $416.50; $1,266.50

  8. $225.50; $1,250.50
  9. $190.00; $990.00
  10. $195.00; $1,695.00
  11. $337.50; $2,587.50
  12. $207.75; $1,592.75

Lesson 5.2, page 64
  1. $96.25; $596.25
  2. $31.50; $211.50
  3. $105.30; $825.30
  4. $110.50; $760.50
  5. $257.40; $842.40
  6. $370.00; $1,970.00
  7. $5.25; $65.25
  8. $136.50; $836.50
  9. $519.75; $2,719.75
  10. $614.25; $1,964.25
  11. $276.00; $676.00
  12. $607.50; $5,607.50

Lesson 5.3, page 65
  1. $31.50; $731.50
  2. $11.25; $511.25
  3. $17.00; $867.00
  4. $19.50; $1,219.50
  5. $12.75; $437.75
  6. $18.00; $218.00
  7. $131.25; $2,631.25
  8. $41.25; $3,041.25
  9. $0.75; $50.75
  10. $59.40; $779.40

Lesson 5.3, page 66
  1. $10.00; $510.00
  2. $65.25; $425.25
  3. $147.00; $747.00
  4. $51.75
  5. $4,462.50; $19,462.50

Posttest, page 67
  1. $36.00; $486.00
  2. $31.50; $661.50
  3. $11.00; $286.00
  4. $35.73; $631.23
  5. $39.60; $399.60
  6. $138.60; $558.60
  7. $262.50; $1,012.50
  8. $56.55; $636.55
  9. $182.00; $1,482.00
  10. $225.25; $1,285.25
  11. $57.75; $657.75
  12. $177.45; $697.45

Grade 7 Answers

13. $28.05; $908.05
14. $30.00; $1,530.00
15. $5.25; $705.25

Posttest, page 68
16. $59.40; $719.40
17. $19.50; $1,219.50
18. $258.75; $1,008.75
19. $189.75; $1,109.75
20. $26.70; $916.70

Chapter 6

Pretest, page 69
	a	b	c
1.	45	1	8
2.	24	5	9
3.	10	16	1
4.	36	3	4
5.	8	11	7

Pretest, page 70
6. 160 7. 12 8. 105 9. 35 10. 56
11. 150 12. 72

Lesson 6.1, page 71
	a	b	c
1.	$\frac{1}{3}$, $\frac{2}{6}$ (circled)	$\frac{3}{8}$, $\frac{1}{4}$	$\frac{3}{5}$, $\frac{9}{15}$ (circled)
2.	$\frac{3}{4}$, $\frac{9}{12}$ (circled)	$\frac{1}{2}$, $\frac{4}{8}$ (circled)	$\frac{5}{6}$, $\frac{15}{18}$ (circled)
3.	$\frac{5}{8}$, $\frac{4}{7}$	$\frac{1}{2}$, $\frac{1}{4}$	$\frac{4}{3}$, $\frac{16}{12}$ (circled)
4.	$\frac{6}{18}$, $\frac{2}{6}$ (circled)	$\frac{3}{25}$, $\frac{6}{50}$ (circled)	$\frac{1}{2}$, $\frac{2}{10}$
5.	$\frac{1}{4}$, $\frac{2}{4}$	$\frac{5}{10}$, $\frac{3}{6}$ (circled)	$\frac{4}{24}$, $\frac{7}{42}$ (circled)
6.	$\frac{3}{5}$, $\frac{5}{3}$	$\frac{7}{8}$, $\frac{21}{24}$ (circled)	$\frac{8}{23}$, $\frac{9}{46}$
7.	$\frac{7}{4}$, $\frac{28}{16}$ (circled)	$\frac{3}{9}$, $\frac{1}{3}$ (circled)	$\frac{16}{20}$, $\frac{9}{10}$
8.	$\frac{8}{100}$, $\frac{80}{50}$	$\frac{8}{12}$, $\frac{10}{14}$	$\frac{15}{20}$, $\frac{3}{4}$ (circled)
9.	$\frac{9}{2}$, $\frac{12}{3}$	$\frac{6}{3}$, $\frac{8}{4}$ (circled)	$\frac{1}{3}$, $\frac{11}{33}$
10.	$\frac{12}{7}$, $\frac{36}{21}$ (circled)	$\frac{10}{12}$, $\frac{15}{20}$	$\frac{3}{4}$, $\frac{9}{16}$

Lesson 6.2, page 72
	a	b	c
1.	8	16	1
2.	9	1	10
3.	21	2	21
4.	64	11	15
5.	15	36	10

Lesson 6.3, page 73
	a	b	c
1.	1	9	8
2.	4	16	5
3.	8	6	6
4.	49	5	10
5.	70	9	10

Lesson 6.4, page 74
1. 64 2. 30 3. 36 4. 7 5. 36 6. 10; 69

Lesson 6.5, page 75
1. 440 2. 8 3. 32 4. 36

Lesson 6.6, page 76
1. 14 2. 3 3. 12 4. 3 5. 8 6. $10 7. 315

Posttest, page 77
	a	b	c
1.	9	2	24
2.	4	25	112
3.	8	6	72
4.	1	3	25
5.	30	16	4

Posttest, page 78
6. 96 7. 72 8. 39 9. 18 10. 36
11. 32 12. 98

Mid-Test

Page 79
	a	b	c	d
1.	525	2210	$13\frac{1}{6}$	$6\frac{11}{40}$
2.	274	361	$2\frac{35}{36}$	$3\frac{1}{14}$
3.	15400	2808	58378	243852
4.	$\frac{5}{24}$	$\frac{1}{4}$	$1\frac{13}{63}$	$\frac{1}{5}$
5.	9	20r4	118r11	169
6.	$1\frac{1}{6}$	$4\frac{1}{5}$	$5\frac{1}{3}$	$2\frac{10}{27}$

Page 80
	a	b	c	d
7.	5355	389023	7.542	34.9562
8.	578441	24092	26.196	6.321
9.	2168.2	1.68	9.1182	289.556
10.	39.2	2368	63.1935	550.68
11.	4	1200	0.8	0.708
12.	5.2	6.15	7.3	3.5

Page 81
	a	b	c
13.	15%	80%	28%
14.	0.3	0.7225	3.46
15.	$\frac{3}{4}$	$\frac{1}{5}$	$1\frac{2}{5}$
16.	2.7	1.2	19.8
17.	82	3	80

18.   25%   4%   95%
19. $93.60; $813.60
20. $96.25; $596.25
21. $1.80; $61.80
22. $315.00; $795.00

Page 82

23. 70   **24.** $60.75; $510.75   **25.** 7
26. $4.05; $184.05   **27.** $384   **28.** $139.50; 18%

Chapter 7

Pretest, page 83

	a	b	c
1.	42	7480	13200
2.	30	27	$1\frac{1}{8}$
3.	50	87	5600
4.	4.575	5 ft. 9 in.	1512
5.	5.5	13	5.125
6.	2.25	53	13 qt. 1 pt.
7.	86	12	22 pt.
8.	9 pt. 1 c.	3 gal. 1 qt.	22 qt.
9.	1.5	1.2	88
10.	12500	208	0.75
11.	3.1	0.75	5200
12.	1 lb. 2 oz.	2 lb. 8 oz.	4
13.	330	$6\frac{1}{3}$	900
14.	4.5	1.2	8 days 12 hr.
15.	9 min. 20 sec.	78	1380
16.	3600	0.75	900

Pretest, page 84

17.   English: 7 hr. 23 min.   Science: 8 hr. 47 min.
      History: 7 hr. 54 min.   Spanish: 7 hr. 18 min.
      Math: 6 hr. 22 min.   Total: 1 day 13 hr. 44 min.
18.   228 oz.; 14.25 lb.
19.   28.5 qt.; 7.125 gal.
20.   3 yd. 1 ft. 6 in.
21.   1.9 mi.

Lesson 7.1, page 85

	a	b	c
1.	51	42240	3
2.	7.8	14960	59
3.	120	37	21120
4.	7222	161	12672
5.	9 yd. 4 in.	73216	12.5
6.	772.8	199584	10871

7. 440   **8.** 200   **9.** 2816 yd.; 8448 ft.

Lesson 7.2, page 86

	a	b	c
1.	6.5	10	14
2.	4.5	9	21.6
3.	24	34	2 gal. 3 qt.
4.	8	84	13 pt. 1 c.
5.	4.75	19	4 gal. 1 pt.

6. 8   **7.** 7   **8.** 168 qt.; 336 pt.

Lesson 7.3, page 87

1.   18 c.; 4.5 qt.; 1.125 gal.
2.   3520 yd.; 10560 ft.; 2 mi.
3.   4 ft. 10 in.; 4 ft. 9 in.; 4 ft. 6 in.; Bill
4.   1.4375   **5.** 6 pt.; 12 c.

Lesson 7.4, page 88

	a	b	c
1.	7000 lb.	4.5 lb.	12 oz.
2.	4.5 T.	2 T.	$26\frac{7}{8}$
3.	5 T. 689 lb.	52 oz.	1.9 T.
4.	158 oz.	12.35 T.	13600 lb.
5.	32 lb. 7 oz.	104 oz.	26000 lb.

6. 1.6 T.   **7.** 204.8 oz.   **8.** 108 oz.; 6.75 lb.

Lesson 7.5, page 89

	a	b	c
1.	0.2 hr.	15 min.	210 min.
2.	192 hr.	420 sec.	3.5 days
3.	5 hr. 20 min.	315 min.	6.6 min.
4.	6 days 6 hr.	$\frac{1}{2}$ hr.	390 min.
5.	1008 hr.	195 min.	225 sec.

6. 1.6 min.   **7.** 1.5 hr.   **8.** 9 days; 12 hr.

Lesson 7.6, page 90

1.   5 min. 24 sec.; 5 min. 48 sec.; 5 min. 22 sec.; Will
2.   11.25 lb.
3.   4.125 gal.; 33 pt.; 66 c.
4.   29000 lb.   **5.** 5.75 days   **6.** 67.2 oz.

Posttest, page 91

	a	b	c
1.	24 yd.	1.5 ft.	2112 yd.
2.	37.5 ft.	3.75 mi.	20 yd. 2 ft.
3.	80 in.	114 ft.	2.25 mi.
4.	5820 yd.	390 in.	27 yd. 2 ft.
5.	8.5 qt.	3 pt.	10.25 gal.
6.	14 c.	11 qt.	53 c.
7.	6 pt. 1 c.	1.75 gal.	4 gal.
8.	4.25 qt.	26 pt.	19 qt.
9.	1.75 lb.	7000 lb.	40 oz.
10.	4.1 T.	179 oz.	3.375 lb.
11.	3 lb. 8 oz.	14500 lb.	2 lb.

Grade 7 Answers

12.	73.6 oz.	5500 lb.	84 oz.
13.	84 hr.	263 min.	375 sec.
14.	3.5 min.	3 days 16 hr.	5.25 hr.
15.	0.75 hr.	192 sec.	0.5 days
16.	402 sec.	8 days 18 hr.	390 min.

Posttest, page 92

17. 3 T. 820 lb. **18.** 2640 yd.; 7920 ft.
19. 180 qt.; 720 c. **20.** 36 c.; 9 qt.; 2.25 gal.
21. 2 hr. 15 min. **22.** 666 in.; 55 ft. 6 in.

Chapter 8

Pretest, page 93

	a	b
1.	4800 m	120 cm
2.	700 mm	2.475 km
3.	30 mm	0.682 m
4.	80.4 cm	13100 m
5.	5.2 m	0.480 km
6.	2400 mg	6.8 MT
7.	12000 g	0.46 g
8.	4860 kg	2700 g
9.	0.743 kg	800 mg
10.	0.375 MT	2.162 g
11.	710 L	0.56 L
12.	0.087 kL	8940 mL
13.	1.720 kL	0.346 L
14.	2.635 L	500000 L
15.	630 mL	0.5 kL

Pretest, page 94

16. 4 cans **17.** 1130 g **18.** 4.458 km
19. 14.7 cm **20.** 4.557 kL **21.** 25
22. 0.723 kg; 723000 mg

Lesson 8.1, page 95

	a	b	c
1.	3500 m	400 cm	1100 mm
2.	2.5 km	5.2 m	130 mm
3.	40 m	500000 mm	2.3 m
4.	327 cm	0.0016 km	1800 cm
5.	7.2 m	86 cm	750 m
6.	136 mm **7.** 11.32 km		

Lesson 8.2, page 96

	a	b
1.	2500 L	17000 mL
2.	0.560 kL	820 mL
3.	0.427 L	1340 L
4.	1.826 kL	0.038 L
5.	7480 mL	0.075 kL
6.	50 **7.** 3.68 kL	

Lesson 8.3, page 97

	a	b
1.	750 g	3.41 MT
2.	0.827 kg	8450 kg
3.	6200 mg	1300 g
4.	0.25 MT	0.63 g
5.	9000 g	800 mg
6.	2.75 kg; 2750 g **7.** 1.316 MT	

Lesson 8.4, page 98

1. 3225 m; 3.225 km **2.** 270 **3.** 3600 kg
4. 1.93 m **5.** 1 bottle **6.** 57.12 g
7. 1 m 55 cm 4 mm; 1 m 54 cm 8 mm; Pablo

Posttest, page 99

	a	b
1.	6.23 m	0.346 km
2.	21.1 cm	8700 m
3.	13 mm	0.512 m
4.	200 mm	3.864 km
5.	3600 m	882 cm
6.	0.422 MT	5.847 g
7.	0.394 kg	240 mg
8.	2910 kg	3120 g
9.	8200 g	0.643 g
10.	9600 mg	3.425 MT
11.	510 mL	0.832 kL
12.	6.235 L	26000L
13.	4.807 kL	0.918L
14.	0.036 kL	6470 mL
15.	680 L	0.39 L

Posttest, page 100

16. 50 **17.** 1 giant box **18.** 50 **19.** 3.5
20. 1.2 kL **21.** 2.844 km **22.** 9.945 L

Chapter 9

Pretest, page 101

1.

Stem	Leaves
6	6 7 8 8 9
7	2 3 3 3 4 9
8	1 2 2 5

Key: 6 | 7 = 67

Grade 7 Answers

2.

Temperature	Frequency	Cumulative Frequency	Relative Frequency
66–70	5	5	33.33%
71–75	5	10	33.33%
76–80	1	11	6.67%
81–85	4	15	26.67%

3.

4.

	a	**b**
5.	74.1	19
	73	85
	73	66

Pretest, page 102

6.

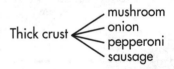

Thin crust — mushroom, onion, pepperoni, sausage

Thick crust — mushroom, onion, pepperoni, sausage

7. 8   **8.** $\frac{1}{2}$ **9.** $\frac{1}{4}$ **10.** $\frac{1}{8}$ **11.** Saturday and Sunday

12. Thursday   **13.** 4   **14.** 90°

15.

Day People Go Grocery Shopping

Lesson 9.1, page 103

1. 85   **2.** 42; 43   **3.** 6   **4.** 11   **5.** 1
6. 6   **7.** cat   **8.** fish   **9.** 10

Lesson 9.2, page 104

1. 11   **2.** 1–5; 21–25; 1   **3.** 11–15   **4.** 2
5. Jan.   **6.** $11\frac{1}{2}$ in.   **7.** $3\frac{1}{2}$ in.   **8.** 2 in.

Lesson 9.3, page 105

1. 36   **2.** 18   **3.** 9   **4.** 2   **5.** 4, 8   **6.** 1, 3
7. strikeouts   **8.** 1

Lesson 9.4, page 106

1. bubblegum   **2.** 40   **3.** 100   **4.** fruit
5. cinnamon and fruit   **6.** 120   **7.** 36°
8. 90°   **9.** 108°

Lesson 9.5, page 107

1. 15 16 17 18 18 20 21 22 23 24
   75 70 75 65 80 75 80 85 80 85
2. negative; no relationship; positive
3.

Note: student answers may vary depending on intervals for axis labels.

Lesson 9.6, page 108

	a	**b**
1.	8	37.1
	9	42.15
	9	23.1
	10	33.6
2.	174.6	516.9
	171	546.25
	171	349
	92	715

Grade 7 Answers

Lesson 9.7, page 109

1.

	a			b	
Stem	Leaves		Stem	Leaves	
1	2 4 6 7 7 8		12	0 2 2	
2	0 1 2 4		13	0 1 2 3 5 5	
3	0 1 3 5		14	2 3 8	

Key: 1|2 = 12   Key: 12|0 = 120

2.

Stem	Leaves		Stem	Leaves
2	1 2		7	3 8
3	2 3		8	2 6
4	5 6		9	3 5
5	1		10	9 9
6	5		11	2

Key: 2|1 = 21   Key: 7|3 = 73

3.

Stem	Leaves		Stem	Leaves
12	8		32	7 9
13	5 7		33	9
14	6		34	2 6 6
15	0 2		35	1
16	4 7		36	8

Key: 12|8 = 128   Key: 32|7 = 327

Lesson 9.8, page 110

	Frequency	Cumulative Frequency	Relative Frequency
1.	3	3	15%
	3	6	15%
	2	8	10%
	4	12	20%
	1	13	5%
	1	14	5%
	2	16	10%
	4	20	20%

2. 4 **3.** 1 **4.** 8 **5.** 7 **6.** 20% **7.** 15%

Lesson 9.9, page 111

1. 15 **2.** 1; 9 **3.** 5 **4.** 9 **5.** 19 **6.** 1½; 3
7. 12 **8.** 0 **9.** 2 or more

Lesson 9.10, page 112

1. 8 **2.** 5; 13 **3.** 63 **4.** 25% **5.** 11 **6.** 18
7. 25% **8.** 22 **9.** 41

Lesson 9.11, page 113

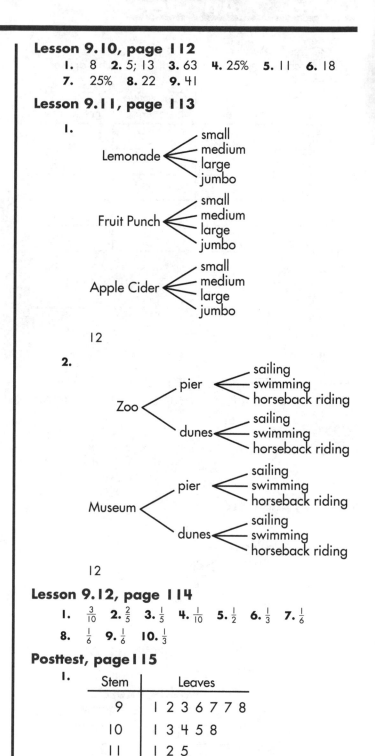

1.

Lemonade — small, medium, large, jumbo

Fruit Punch — small, medium, large, jumbo

Apple Cider — small, medium, large, jumbo

12

2.

Zoo — pier — sailing, swimming, horseback riding; dunes — sailing, swimming, horseback riding

Museum — pier — sailing, swimming, horseback riding; dunes — sailing, swimming, horseback riding

12

Lesson 9.12, page 114

1. $\frac{3}{10}$ **2.** $\frac{2}{5}$ **3.** $\frac{1}{5}$ **4.** $\frac{1}{10}$ **5.** $\frac{1}{2}$ **6.** $\frac{1}{3}$ **7.** $\frac{1}{6}$
8. $\frac{1}{6}$ **9.** $\frac{1}{6}$ **10.** $\frac{1}{3}$

Posttest, page 115

1.

Stem	Leaves
9	1 2 3 6 7 7 8
10	1 3 4 5 8
11	1 2 5

Key: 9|1 = 91

2. Note: Answers will vary depending on intervals chosen in column 1. Here is one possible answer.

Cars	Frequency	Cumulative Frequency	Relative Frequency
91–95	3	3	20%
96–100	4	7	26.67%
101–105	4	11	26.67%
106–110	1	12	6.67%
111–115	3	15	20%

3.

4.

	a	b
5.	101.5	24
	101	108
	97	96

Posttest, page 116

6.

Racing — red, black, silver

Mountain — red, black, silver

7. 6 **8.** $\frac{1}{2}$ **9.** $\frac{1}{3}$ **10.** $\frac{1}{6}$ **11.** 4 **12.** 72°

13. 4–6 **14.** 0–3

15.

Weekly Exercise

Number of People vs. Hours (0–3, 4–6, 7–9, 10–12)

Chapter 10

Pretest, page 117

	a	b	c
1.	point T	$\overline{RS}$ or $\overline{SR}$	$\overleftrightarrow{XY}$ or $\overleftrightarrow{YX}$
2.	$\overrightarrow{DC}$	$\overleftrightarrow{JK}$ or $\overleftrightarrow{KJ}$	$\overline{QR}$ or $\overline{RQ}$
3.	$\angle RST$ or $\angle TSR$	$\overrightarrow{SR}$, $\overrightarrow{ST}$	S
4.	$\angle ABC$ or $\angle CBA$	$\overrightarrow{BA}$, $\overrightarrow{BC}$	B
5.	$\overleftrightarrow{AB}$ and $\overleftrightarrow{CD}$		

6. 60° **7.** acute **8.** ∠9 **9.** ∠5 or ∠7

10. $\overleftrightarrow{RS}$; alternate exterior

11. $\overleftrightarrow{TU}$; alternate interior

12. $\overleftrightarrow{AB}$; alternate exterior

13. $\overleftrightarrow{TU}$; corresponding

Pretest, page 118

	a	b	c
14.	right, isosceles	acute, equilateral	obtuse, scalene
15.	trapezoid	octagon	rectangle
16.	pentagon	hexagon	parallelogram

17. reflection **18.** (4, −1) **19.** (−4, 5) **20.** U

21. N **22.** III **23.** yes

Lesson 10.1, page 119

	a	b
1.	RS ; SR	$\overleftrightarrow{RS}$; $\overleftrightarrow{SR}$
2.	PQ ; QP	$\overleftrightarrow{PQ}$; $\overleftrightarrow{QP}$
3.	MN ; NM	$\overleftrightarrow{MN}$; $\overleftrightarrow{NM}$

	a	b	c
4.	XY; YX	$\overline{XY}$; $\overline{YX}$	X; Y
5.	AB; BA	$\overline{AB}$; $\overline{BA}$	A; B
6.	CD; DC	$\overline{CD}$; $\overline{DC}$	C; D

7–9 Answers will vary. Sample answers are shown.

	a	b
7.	$\overline{T\ U}$	$\overleftrightarrow{O\ P}$
8.	$\overrightarrow{G\ H}$	$\overleftrightarrow{J\ K}$
9.	$\overline{X\ Y}$	$\overleftrightarrow{W\ X}$

Grade 7 Answers

Lesson 10.2, page 120

	a	**b**
1.	AB ; $\overrightarrow{AB}$	A
2.	CD ; $\overrightarrow{CD}$	C
3.	FE ; $\overrightarrow{FE}$	F
4.	GHI ; IHG $\quad$ $\angle GHI$ $\angle IHG$	
	$\overrightarrow{HG}$; $\overrightarrow{HI}$	H
5.	JKL ; LKJ $\quad$ $\angle JKL$ $\angle LKJ$	
	$\overrightarrow{KJ}$; $\overrightarrow{KL}$	K
6.	MNO ; ONM $\angle MNO$ $\angle ONM$	
	$\overrightarrow{NM}$; $\overrightarrow{NO}$	N

7.

8.

Lesson 10.3, page 121

	a	**b**
1.	$60°$; acute	$90°$; right
2.	$120°$; obtuse	$30°$; acute
3.	$140°$; obtuse	$80°$; acute

Lesson 10.4, page 122

1. $\angle GHJ$ or $\angle GHM$
2. $\angle FHG$
3. $\angle JMK$ or $\angle IMH$
4. $\overrightarrow{ML}$
5. $\angle CFD$
6. $\angle GFE$
7. $77°$
8. $68°$
9. $52°$; $104°$

Lesson 10.5, page 123

1. $\overleftrightarrow{RS}$; corresponding
2. $\overleftrightarrow{AB}$; alternate interior
3. $\overleftrightarrow{RS}$; corresponding
4. $\overleftrightarrow{TU}$; alternate exterior
5. $\overleftrightarrow{TU}$; alternate interior

6. $\overleftrightarrow{CD}$; alternate exterior
7. $\overleftrightarrow{TU}$; alternate exterior
8. $\overleftrightarrow{TU}$; corresponding
9. $\overleftrightarrow{AB}$; alternate interior
10. $\overleftrightarrow{CD}$; alternate interior
11. $\overleftrightarrow{RS}$; corresponding
12. $\overleftrightarrow{TU}$; corresponding

Lesson 10.6, page 124

	a	**b**	**c**
1.	acute	right	acute
2.	obtuse	obtuse	right
3.	obtuse	acute	right
4.	right	obtuse	acute

Lesson 10.7, page 125

	a	**b**	**c**
1.	scalene	equilateral	scalene
2.	isosceles	scalene	isosceles
3.	equilateral	scalene	isosceles

Lesson 10.8, page 126

1. rectangle and square
2. rhombus and square
3. no
4. yes
5. yes
6. no
7. yes

	a	**b**
8.	trapezoid	square, rhombus, rectangle, parallelogram
9.	parallelogram	rectangle, parallelogram

Lesson 10.9, page 127

	a	**b**
1.	heptagon	decagon
2.	nonagon	pentagon
3.	octagon	hexagon
4.	heptagon	nonagon

Lesson 10.10, page 128

	a	**b**
1.	$\frac{AB}{XY} = \frac{BC}{YZ}$ $\frac{1}{2} = \frac{1}{2}$ similar	$\frac{AB}{WX} = \frac{BC}{XY}$ $\frac{2.3}{1.5} \neq \frac{1.5}{1}$ not similar
2.	$\frac{AB}{TU} = \frac{BC}{UV} = \frac{CD}{VW} = \frac{DE}{WX} = \frac{EA}{XT}$	$\frac{AB}{WX} = \frac{BC}{XY} = \frac{CD}{YZ} = \frac{DA}{ZW}$
	$\frac{2}{3} = \frac{2}{3} \neq \frac{1}{2} \neq \frac{1}{1} \neq \frac{1}{2}$ not similar	$\frac{6}{3} = \frac{12}{6} = \frac{10}{5} = \frac{5}{2.5}$ similar

Grade 7 Answers

Lesson 10.11, page 129

	a	b
1.	D	A
2.	E	C
3.	F	B
4.	(−4, 3)	(−4, −2)
5.	(−2, −3)	(1, −3)
6.	(2, 1)	(2, 3)

7–9. See grid for points A, B, C, D, E, and F.

Lesson 10.12, page 130

	a	b	c
1.	translation	translation	reflection
2.	reflection	dilation	rotation
3.	translation	rotation	dilation

Posttest, page 131

	a	b	c
1.	$\overline{MN}$ or $\overline{NM}$	point P	$\overleftrightarrow{KL}$ or $\overleftrightarrow{LK}$
2.	$\overrightarrow{XY}$	$\overline{RS}$ or $\overline{SR}$	$\overrightarrow{FG}$
3.	$\angle TUV$ or $\angle VUT$	$\overrightarrow{UT}$, $\overrightarrow{UV}$	U
4.	$\angle HIJ$ or $\angle JIH$	$\overrightarrow{IH}$, $\overrightarrow{IJ}$	I

5. $\angle 8$ **6.** $\angle 10$ or $\angle 12$

7. $\overleftrightarrow{WX}$ and $\overleftrightarrow{YZ}$

8. 110° **9.** obtuse

10. $\overleftrightarrow{PQ}$; alternate exterior

11. $\overleftrightarrow{RS}$; corresponding

12. $\overleftrightarrow{YZ}$; alternate interior

Posttest, page 132

	a	b	c
13.	acute, isosceles	right, scalene	obtuse, scalene
14.	square	pentagon	decagon
15.	rhombus	heptagon	hexagon

16. slide **17.** rotation **18.** (3, −2) **19.** I

20. B **21.** (−3, 1)

22. yes; $\frac{AB}{GH} = \frac{BC}{HI} = \frac{CA}{IG}$

Chapter 11

Pretest, page 133

	a	b	c
1.	10 yd.	11.3 cm	35 ft.
2.	21 cm	12 m	8 in.
3.	50.24 m	43.96 ft.	232.36 yd.
4.	28.26 sq. cm	133 sq. in.	200.96 sq. mm

Pretest, page 134

5. 124 sq. m; 72 cubic m

6. 390 sq. in.; 378 cubic in.

7. 130.5 sq. cm; 85 cubic cm

8. 1435 sq. ft.; 2992 cubic ft.

	a	b	c
9.	252 cubic ft.	360 cubic m	25 cubic yd.

10. 6 ft.; 263.76 sq. ft.; 310.86 cubic ft.

11. 9 cm; 791.28 sq. cm; 1271.7 cubic cm

12. 5 m; 290.45 sq. m; 314 cubic m

13. 19 in.; 6085.32 sq. in.; 36273.28 cubic in.

Lesson 11.1, page 135

	a	b	c
1.	14 ft.	13 yd.	12.5 m
2.	$7\frac{1}{4}$	64 cm	45 yd.
3.	44 ft.	9 m	12 in.
4.	12 m	19.2 cm	80 yd.

Lesson 11.2, page 136

	a	b	c
1.	18 sq. yd.	324 sq. m	276 sq. cm
2.	216 sq. km	529 sq. in.	48 sq. ft.
3.	9 in.	13 ft.	9 m
4.	13 cm	75 m	36.8 yd.

Lesson 11.3, page 137

	a	b	c
1.	27.5 sq. ft.	48 sq. yd.	104.5 sq. in.
2.	10 sq. ft.	123.25 sq. cm	32 sq. m
3.	1330 sq. mm	378 sq. in.	10.5 sq. yd.

Grade 7 Answers

Lesson 11.4, page 138

1. 138 ft. **2.** 108 sq. in. **3.** 12 m **4.** 54 in.
5. 1271 sq. cm **6.** $10\frac{5}{8}$ **7.** 8 in.; 8 in.

Lesson 11.5, page 139

	a	b	c
1.	1.5 ft.	0.75 ft.	
2.		1.75 m	10.99 m
3.	6.5 in.		20.41 in.
4.	8.5 yd.	4.25 yd.	
5.		3.75 cm	23.55 cm
6.	30 in.		94.2 in.
7.	2.5 m	1.25 m	
8.		2.5 km	15.7 km
9.	10 ft.	5 ft.	
10.	90 cm		282.6 cm
11.		2 yd.	12.56 yd.
12.	3 mi.	1.5 mi.	

Lesson 11.6, page 140

	a	b	c
1.	50.2 sq. ft.	113 sq. m	530.7 sq. cm
2.	1017.4 sq. yd.	452.2 sq. km	153.9 sq. in.
3.	6 in.		28.3 sq. in.
4.		9 ft.	254.3 sq. ft.
5.		8.5 m	226.9 sq. m
6.	64 cm		3215.4 sq. cm
7.		15 km	706.5 sq. km
8.	12 yd.		113 sq. yd.

Lesson 11.7, page 141

	a	b	c
1.	52 sq. ft.	48 sq. m	24 sq. cm
2.	185 sq. yd.	9 sq. mi.	20 sq. in.
3.	25 sq. ft.	72 sq. in.	77 sq. cm

Lesson 11.8, page 142

	a	b	c
1.	62 sq. in.	48.7 sq. ft.	172 sq. yd.
2.	856 sq. cm	104 sq. m	248 sq. in.
3.	85.5 sq. ft.	2970 sq. mm	81.44 sq. cm

Lesson 11.9, page 143

	a	b	c
1.	18 cubic ft.	16 cubic m	135 cubic in.
2.	672 cubic cm	28 cubic yd.	672 cubic ft.
3.	27 cubic in.	10.5 cubic m	1035 cubic cm

Lesson 11.10, page 144

1. 7.85 in. **2.** 2289.06 sq. cm **3.** 76.5 sq. in.
4. 404 sq. m **5.** 30000 cubic cm **6.** 252 sq. in.

Lesson 11.11, page 145

	a	b	c
1.	1485 cubic in.	15 cubic m	22.5 cubic cm
2.	63 cubic ft.	3.75 cubic yd.	12.8 cubic in.
3.	3.9375 cubic m	15.456 cubic ft.	96.32 cubic cm

Lesson 11.12, page 146

	a	b	c
1.	376.8 sq. in.	1055.04 sq. ft.	5224.96 sq. mm
2.	37.68 sq. yd.	596.6 sq. cm	1004.8 sq. ft.
3.	173.328 sq. m	1099 sq. in.	2417.8 sq. cm

Lesson 11.13, page 147

	a	b	c
1.	16076.8 cubic in.	3538.78 cubic cm	747.7596 cubic ft.
2.	1582.56 cubic m	8440.32 cubic mm	87.92 cubic in.
3.	26660.013 cubic mm	2034.72 cubic yd.	4876.9224 cubic cm

Lesson 11.14, page 148

1. 13.5 cubic m **2.** 40 cubic cm **3.** 2 in.
4. 593.46 sq. cm; 1049.1525 cubic cm
5. 252.77 sq. in.; 307.72 cubic in.
6. 104.248 sq. m; 79.128 cubic m

Posttest, page 149

	a	b	c
1.	12 m	16 ft.	20 cm
2.	36 in.	20 yd.	55 mm
3.	81.64 m	56.52 cm	21.98 ft.
4.	63.585 sq. in.	75 sq. m	28 sq. yd.
5.	169 sq. cm	1296 sq. ft.	452.16 sq. mm

Posttest, page 150

	a	b	
6.	122 sq. yd.	72 cubic yd.	
7.	45 sq. m	18 cubic m	
8.	1976 sq. mm	5796 cubic mm	
9.	93 sq. in.	45 cubic in.	

	a	b	c
10.	3024 cubic in.	180 cubic cm	38.25 cubic m
11.	1.5 m	89.49 sq. m	56.52 cubic m
12.	4 yd.	113.04 sq. yd.	87.92 cubic yd.
13.	11 in.	3108.6 sq. in.	12917.96 cubic in.
14.	14 cm	439.6 sq. cm	461.58 cubic cm

Grade 7 Answers

Chapter 12

Pretest, page 151

	a	b
1.	$n - 5$	$b + 8$
2.	$n \div 6$	$2 \times n$
3.	$3 + n = 12$	$x - 6 = 19$
4.	$30 \div n = 3$	$5 \times n = 15$

	a	b	c
5.	6	9	12
6.	15	4	22
7.	14	12	16
8.	17	4	0
9.	5	6	7
10.	3	4	6
11.	36	42	14
12.	18	60	72

Pretest, page 152

	a	b	c
13.	5	24	20
14.	8	8	5
15.	-1	1	3
16.	-11	-1	-13
17.	-6	7	-6
18.	-5	9	-1
19.	-42	-12	10
20.	-20	16	-24
21.	-3	3	-3
22.	3	-5	-3
23.	243	64	64
24.	25	64	4096
25.	0.0625	0.33333	0.0016
26.	0.11111	0.16666	0.25

Lesson 12.1, page 153

1a. variable expression **1b.** equation **1c.** inequality
2a. numerical expression **2b.** inequality
2c. equation

	a	b
3.	$d + 3$	$8 \times w$
4.	$12 - 7$	$n + 2$
5.	$n \div 6$	$15 + 9$
6.	$5 + 6 = 11$	$12 \div s = 4$
7.	$t - 3 > 5$	$2 \times b > 4$
8.	$5 \times 3 = y$	$20 \div n = 5$

Lesson 12.2, page 154

	a	b
1.	commutative	associative
2.	identity	commutative
3.	associative	zero
4.	identity	commutative
5.	zero	associative
6.	$3 + (7 + y)$	642
7.	$z \times 15$	0
8.	$12a$	$(14 \times 3) \times p$
9.	0	$16 + 49$
10.	$d + 3$	$6 \times (4 \times n)$

Lesson 12.3, page 155

	a	b
1.	$a \times (4 + 3)$	$(b \times 6) + (b \times 12)$
2.	$(4 \times a) + (4 \times b)$	$3 \times (a + b)$
3.	$d \times (5 - 2)$	$(5 \times 8) + (5 \times p)$
4.	$(d \times 8) - (d \times h)$	$(12 \times s) - (12 \times 10)$
5.	$(r \times 16) + (r \times s)$	$35 \times (t + y)$
6.	$8 \times (a + b)$	$(r \times q) - (r \times s)$
7.	$6 \times (12 - w)$	$(p \times 15) + (p \times z)$
8.	$(15 \times y) + (15 \times 0)$	$d \times (d + b)$
9.	$a \times (2 + 3 + 4)$	$(p \times a) + (p \times b) + (p \times 4)$
10.	$a \times (b + c - d)$	$(8 \times a) + (8 \times b) + (8 \times c)$

Lesson 12.4, page 156

	a	b	c
1.	16	11	19
2.	17	33	2
3.	9	28	28
4.	36	3	7
5.	14	5	4
6.	1	4	2
7.	7	5	10
8.	18	5	45
9.	7	11	17
10.	6	3	5
11.	9	9	7
12.	6	12	8
13.	16	32	140
14.	11	43	17

Lesson 12.5, page 157

	a	b	c
1.	7	6	15
2.	14	2	22
3.	33	13	0
4.	23	0	15
5.	14	24	1
6.	6	6	24

7. $21 + n = 37$; 16
8. $n - 9 = 33$; 42
9. $2 + 5 + n = 25$; 18

Grade 7 Answers

Lesson 12.6, page 158

	a	b	c
1.	9	5	6
2.	12	27	15
3.	8	1	6
4.	50	36	48
5.	5	0	16
6.	19	28	63

7. $6 \times n = 12$ or $12 \div 6 = n$; 2
8. $48 \div n = 12$ or $48 \div 12 = n$; 4
9. $25 \times n = 150$ or $150 \div 25 = n$; 6

Lesson 12.7, page 159

	a	b	c	d
1.	8	5	−2	5
2.	−8	3	−10	10
3.	3	−9	−1	−23
4.	−15	1	−5	−11
5.	−16	−11	2	−5
6.	−15	−10	43	−15
7.	−9	1	−1	0
8.	0	−11	−4	−1
9.	0	−3	−10	11
10.	7	9	−16	4

Lesson 12.8, page 160

	a	b	c	d
1.	6	−24	−24	12
2.	3	−4	−2	−3
3.	−56	−30	24	−44
4.	−7	−2	−4	4
5.	−32	4	−88	70
6.	−27	−7	11	2
7.	40	−36	26	−81
8.	−3	−19	19	−7
9.	−17	−10	−42	35
10.	−1	−2	6	−9

Lesson 12.9, page 161

	a	b	c
1.	49	512	64
2.	100	6561	161051
3.	4913	15625	1296
4.	9261	65536	248832
5.	8^5; 32768	3^6; 729	2^4; 16
6.	7^2; 49	9^2; 81	16^2; 256
7.	6^5; 7776	4^6; 4096	3^4; 81
8.	10^2; 100	8^1; 8	7^3; 343
9.	5^5; 3125	10^7; 10000000	15^3; 3375
10.	2^5; 32	3^2; 9	6^3; 216

Lesson 12.10, page 162

	a	b	c
1.	$\frac{1}{3^2}$; 0.1111	$\frac{1}{6^3}$; 0.0046	$\frac{1}{8^2}$; 0.0156
2.	$\frac{1}{7^3}$; 0.0029	$\frac{1}{3^3}$; 0.0370	$\frac{1}{9^2}$; 0.0123
3.	$\frac{1}{4^3}$; 0.0156	$\frac{1}{5^2}$; 0.04	$\frac{1}{2^3}$; 0.125
4.	$\frac{1}{2^4}$; 0.0625	$\frac{1}{10^3}$; 0.001	$\frac{1}{1^4}$; 1
5.	0.00098	0.03125	0.00412
6.	0.00077	0.00006	0.01235
7.	0.01563	0.00292	0.125
8.	0.0625	0.01563	0.03704
9.	0.0625	0.04	0.00463
10.	0.00412	0.00391	0.125

Posttest, page 163

	a	b
1.	$n - 7$	$n + 8$
2.	$6 \times n$	$n \div 12$
3.	$4 \times n = 16$	$n + 9 = 11$
4.	$n - 3 = 20$	$25 \div b = 5$

	a	b	c
5.	7	5	21
6.	12	18	12
7.	5	8	11
8.	1	4	6
9.	9	5	5
10.	5	31	6
11.	33	54	16
12.	28	21	24

Posttest, page 164

	a	b	c
13.	6	15	16
14.	8	6	2
15.	−2	4	−7
16.	3	−3	−12
17.	−3	17	−10
18.	−3	15	−10
19.	−12	−18	16
20.	30	−63	6
21.	−2	−4	10
22.	−1	−17	−23
23.	16	243	216
24.	49	512	125
25.	0.03704	0.03125	0.0625
26.	0.33333	0.00292	0.25

Grade 7 Answers

Final Test

Page 165

	a	b	c	d
1.	$\frac{3}{40}$	$\frac{2}{7}$	$1\frac{27}{28}$	$3\frac{5}{24}$
2.	$\frac{11}{16}$	$2\frac{6}{7}$	$15\frac{1}{6}$	$\frac{29}{36}$
3.	$1\frac{5}{7}$	$\frac{6}{7}$	$1\frac{7}{8}$	$2\frac{7}{9}$
4.	$2\frac{8}{15}$	$1\frac{7}{27}$	$32\frac{1}{2}$	$1\frac{1}{6}$

5. $21; $371
6. $113.40; $833.40
7. $56.95; $1396.95
8. $85.50; $685.50

	a	b	c
9.	12	4	8
10.	24	32	36

Page 166

	a	b	c
11.	5720 yd.	63 in.	56 oz.
12.	$3\frac{1}{4}$ days	3 hr. 43 min.	14 pt.
13.	0.340 km	70 cm	1200 mg
14.	0.350 kL	1.246 kg	1.382 L

15. **Quiz Scores**

Stem	Leaves
0	8 9 9
1	0 1 2 3 4 5 6 7 7 8
2	0 1 2 2 2 3 3

Key: 0 | 8 = 8

16. **Quiz Scores**

17. 16.1; 22
    16.5; 15
18. 25% **19.** 23 **20.** 8 **21.** 30%

Page 167

	a	b	c
22.	20 yd.	17 m	28 in.
23.	126 sq. cm	324 sq. mm	176 sq. ft.
24.	50.24 cm	37.68 in.	113.04 yd.
	200.96 sq. cm	113.04 sq. in.	1017.36 sq. yd.
25.	812 sq. in.	2512 sq. ft.	182 sq. cm
26.	339.12 cubic in.	313.5 cubic cm	60 cubic m

Page 168

	a	b	c
27.	17	4	19
28.	17	18	8
29.	6	3	11
30.	25	40	60
31.	50	6	34
32.	−2	−5	−1
33.	−14	−3	26
34.	−12	−12	27
35.	−2	−2	7
36.	−10	−5	−10
37.	8	81	32
38.	0.03125	0.33333	0.25
39.	−1	0	−6
40.	13	4	7